Stranger in my House

Ashley S. Henry

ISBN: 1481149660
ISBN-13: 978-1481149662

DEDICATION

My family

ACKNOWLEDGMENTS

Thanks to my family and friends.

"Mrs. Washington, Darrell is on line one." I heard my secretary say through the intercom.

"Okay, thank you Shardae." I looked up at the silver plated digital clock that hung on the wall above my office door.

Eleven-thirty.

It was Darrell's daily call to make sure that I would be able to meet him for lunch at '*Red Lobster;*' the same place that we've been meeting since we meet four years ago.

"Hey baby, I'll be there waiting for you." I said, excited that we would finally be spending some time together.

"Yeah, about that; I won't be able to make it today," the smile that was plastered on my mahogany colored face fell.

"That's the third time this week you've cancelled on me Darrell." I took the phone off of speaker and leaned back in my chair closing my eyes. I was ready to listen to another one of his lame excuses.

"I have to work through lunch to have this case ready Monday morning." Darrell explained. "I'll see you when I get home tonight."

"And what time will that be?"

"I don't know Joi, but I'll call if I'm going to be late."

"Yeah, I'll see you in the morning as you're leaving out for work."

"Aight, whateva. I'll call you lata, I gotta go." There was no *'bye'* or *'I love you'* before he hung up, he just, hung up. I rolled my eyes refusing to allow him to ruin my day.

I was born as Keyna Graham twenty-six years ago. Two months later my name had changed to Joi Young by my adopted parents. They said that they knew I was going to be bringing them so much *joy* into their life from the first time they laid eyes on me. I grew up in a middle class family, youngest of three; I was spoiled by my parents. If there was anything that I wanted, I'd get it. Some people would call me boogie and some would call me stuck up, and growing up with those names on my back I learned to embrace it. Call me what you want, I'd still look and be fabulous.

I met Darrell back when the social networking sites were real big. It was the summer I graduated from High School. I was scrolling through the list of kids that I went to middle school with when I came across Darrell's profile. I was hesitant to communicate with him, but I thought what the heck, the most he could do was internet stock me; so I sent him a message asking how he was doing and seeing how life had treated him. From that one message we started talking every day and having those late night conversations. After a month we finally decided to meet up. He looked like Musiq Soulchild except for the eye thing Musiq has going on. Darrell and I were what some people may say, made for each other. We both liked the best things in life, never settled for less.

Two years of dating we found out that we were going to be bringing a baby into this world. Within that same year of graduating we had gotten married, and I had become the new Mrs. Joi Washington. Of course some people figured we were moving too fast, but when you're in love why wait? After graduating Maryland University I started my own publishing company, *'I Got Flow'* publishing. Darrell was becoming one of the best public defender lawyers in the DC area.

We lived in a nice four bedroom house in

Upper Marlboro Maryland, away from the ghetto that the both of us had grew up in. Like any other marriage we'd had our share of problems; but for the past year it has went downhill. Half the time we weren't speaking and when we were, we're arguing about something. Our daughter, Camille, was the only thing keeping us together.

*

"Sorry I'm late," I said as I got to the table interrupting my girls from talking.

"Hey Missy Poo," Malikaa said with a wide grin spread across her face. I smiled back at her as I sat down. Malikaa was the model type chick but too short to be 'America's Next Top Model.' If height wasn't the issue she would surely win. She only stood at five-one, two inches taller than me, butter peacan skin, never showed her natural hair, she was what I called the wig queen; a wig for every occasion. She was the mother of the group but had no children. She had it all going for herself. No children, a bachelor's degree in criminal justice, and works as a lawyer's assistant downtown. She was working on her master's degree until she met Rashaad. I knew he was trouble from the first time she introduced us to him. My gut feelings were right because now he's down in Virginia serving a three year sentence.

"So, what I miss? Did ya'll order yet?" I questioned as I picked up my menu and looked at it.

"If you were here on time you wouldn't have missed anything." That was Yasmine. "Sike nah, hi Joi," she smiled. "Why are you late?" If I had to pick a television personality to describe her I would say she was Mya off of the television show *'Girlfriends.'* Yasmine was quite pretty herself. Hair flowing down her back, her hair. Not the 16in' that you get from Ming Lee. Beautiful brown skin with Asian slanted eyes. Her skin was flawless, she had the occasional pimple her and there but nothing heavy. She was thick, not fat, but thick. Of course she had her mommy pouch that she inherited after she had Isaac, but I believe she was working on it.

"If you must know I was getting it in," I smiled at them. Yasmine threw me a smirk as Malikaa said, "I know that's right."

"Yup, well, what were you ladies smiling about when I walked up?" I picked up my menu and began scanning for a meal that was affordable yet something that sticks to my diet.

"Oh, we were just talking about last weekend." Malikaa told me smiling ear from ear. I raised my eyebrow showing that I still was unclear as to what they were laughing at. "Oh, yeah that's right, you weren't with us."

"Uh, no; what happened last weekend?" before they had a chance to respond I blurted out, "Oh, I think I want salmon and rice tonight. Oh, no I can't do rice. I got a taste for broccoli."

"Well get broccoli," Yasmine said.

"I know, I think I just might do that. Anyway, what ya'll do last weekend?"

"We went to *Buffalo Wild Wings* right, and we were having a nice little time watching the fight. Then this guy gonna come up to Yesi and try to spit his little game, but why when he asked for her number she gonna ask *'What you want my number for?'* you had to be there because her facial expression was priceless."

"No, let me tell you, we were at the table talking. Malikaa and I, I kept seeing the guy looking at us while we were talking so I'm telling her cause I'm trying to figure out why is he looking at us when he has a girl sitting in front of him. The nigga was showing me his phone, so I'm thinking he bold to be doing that with his girl in front of him, I ignore him. So me and Malikaa still talking when I see the girl get up from the table." I interrupted her.

"What girl?" Yasmine sucked her teeth.

"Are you listening, the girl that was sitting with the guy that was starring at us."

"Oh okay, go ahead."

"So she got up from the table and he came over to us and he started conversating with me."

"Conversating isn't a word, but go ahead." I cut her off. She smacked her lips.

"Then he asked me for my number, so that's when I asked him why he wanted my number. Him and Malikaa looked at me like I was crazy, so I asked if that was his girlfriend that was just sitting at the table and he said no it was his sister. I was reassured when she came back from where ever she went and stood beside him."

"So did you get his number, or give him yours?" I asked.

"I sure did, he looked good." Yasmine said with a smile spread across her face. We all laughed. We waved our waitress over to us and ordered our food. While waiting for our food we sat and talked out some of our problems and talked about our past.

We finished eating and catching up and waved down our waitress. After paying for our meal we gathered our things and walked outside. The muggy air stuck to my face like Velcro, I immediately felt dirty. We walked until we got to Yasmine's car.

"Have any of you talked to Lisa?" Malikaa asked as she picked at her nails.

"I haven't heard from her." I told them.

"I'm worried about her. I only talked to her once, and that was about a week after she up and disappeared." Malikaa said before taking a long drag out of her cigarette and flicking her cancer stick across the parking lot.

"I wonder why she picked up and left like that," I said to no one in particular. Lisa, better known as Jalissa Mitchell was the fourth person in the group. Three years ago, the day after my wedding, she packed up all of her things and left. No one knew where she had gone. She had us all worried sick because we had no clue as to where she had gone. After having called the police, and having her put out as a missing person she finally called two weeks later. She didn't mention where she was, just told us that she was okay and not to worry. We weren't really on speaking terms seeing that our friendship was falling apart, but Yasmine said that once or twice a month she would get a letter with no return address on it from her or a phone call from her.

"I talked to her last week," we looked to Yasmine.

"What she say?" Malikaa asked.

"Nothing, just catching up; she was asking me how everyone was. Asking about her mom and brothers and Jamie."

"Did she tell you where she was?" I can tell that she was debating on telling us.

"No she didn't tell me; but I know she's somewhere in Chicago."

"Chicago, how you know?" Malikaa questioned.

"Because I listened and paid attention when she talked while she was home," I gave her this uh huh look. She returned a stink look and rolled her eyes.

"Well, I gota go ya'll. Call me later cause its hot out here I have to go and get the kids from my mom's house." Yasmine said. We said our good-byes and went our separate ways.

Yasmine

"Xavier, get your ass in here now!" I yelled. It was the third time this month his teacher has called the house and I was tired of it. I didn't want to whoop him because quite frankly I was tired of beating him. It seems as if he wasn't getting it. Xavier was my eldest son and my most troubled one. He was seven years old, and a splitting image of his father. He had his father's attitude and everything else that resembled that man.

Xavier walked into my room with his head into his Nintendo DS. I immediately snatched it out of his hand. He looked up at me with a puzzled look on his face.

"What I do?" he asked me.

"What happened in school today?" he looked at me with a dumbfounded look. The same look his father gives. "Why you get in trouble at school today Xavier?"

"Cause I was talking in class and I didn't complete my work," he said so low that I could barely hear him. I popped him in the mouth. He quickly covered his mouth and backed away from me.

"What I tell you about running your mouth in school," he shrugged his shoulders. "You know what I told you. What I say?"

"You said to shut my mouth and stop trying to be the class clown." He leaned against my wall across from me.

"So why can't you do that?" he shrugged his shoulders again. "I don't understand that,"

"I don't know,"

"Because you don't know you're not to go outside, watch T.V. or play any of those video games." I told him.

"Until when?" He questioned me.

"Until I say so, get in that damn room and look at the four walls for entertainment." He put his head down and walked out of the room. It was these times when I really needed Robert, his father, to step up and really be in his life. I took care of the two boys the best I could, but they needed that father to knock some good discipline into their heads.

I had met Robert through Jalissa. I had needed a date for our senior prom and she suggested her cousin. We made ourselves an official couple prom night; both of us scared to tell Jalissa the news. Until this day we have no idea why we were so scared. Robert was my *first* true love. I thought about him and his well-being every waking hour. We had the craziest times when we were in the middle of falling in love. I would never forget the time when he ran in my house screaming and panicking, "Omg Yesi! It hurt, Omg!" he shouted as he walked back and forth across the room with his hand covering his eye. I began to panic.

"What? What what's wrong? Calm down," I shouted for him trying to get him to calm down so he could tell me what's going on with him.

"Yasmine my eye!" he continued to shout.

"What's wrong with your eye?" by then I was frantic as I tried to remove his hand from his face. He would not budge.

"A bee stung me." I stopped and looked at him. Fits of laughter emerged from out of my mouth.

"A bee Rob, you over here crying over a bee?" I laughed him out for the rest of the day.

Our days changed once I had become pregnant with Xavier. Everything began to come to light, all of his cheating and secret relationships. And like a fool I stayed there, good dick always finds a way to keep you further in, because I had gotten pregnant again with Isaac.

I stood in the kitchen flipping the fried chicken that I was cooking for dinner when I heard my cell phone ringing to Bobby Valention's *Anonymous*. By the tune that was playing I knew it was a caller that I didn't know or I don't really talk to. I wasn't going to worry about answering the phone but then I remembered that Robert had a tendency to call me from random numbers. I ran into my room to answer my phone. I didn't recognize the number, but I answered anyway.

"Hello," I spoke.

"Can I speak to Yesi," a man with a profound voice asked.

"Who is this?" I asked. I didn't know too many males who call my phone from a number that I didn't know.

"Adrian, I met you at the Buffalo Wild Wings about a week ago," I kept saying his name in my head, as I walked back into the kitchen, until a face came with the name.

"Oh, okay. Hey, how are you?" I asked.

"I'm doing good, been working like a Hebrew slave." What he said wasn't funny, but I gave a slight laugh just to please his sense of humor. "So how are you?"

"I've been good, just doing me. What type of work do you do?" I asked as I began to make the mashed potatoes.

"I do construction, what do you do?"

"I'm a nurse," I told him. He began coughing. "Um,"

"I think I'm coming down with something, can you come and nurse me back to health." I burst into laughter.

"Oh my God, that was so corny." He laughed as well.

"Damn, corny though,"

"Yes corny, don't ever use that line to any female anymore." We both laughed again.

"Aight, so Ms. Yesi, tell me about you," and that I did. I told him all the things that I thought he should know. We talked for about an hour and the half just getting to know one another. I looked at the clock and noticed that it was nine o'clock and time for me to get Issac, my youngest son, and Xavier ready for bed. I ended the phone call by promising that I would call him when I got the kids to bed. I was so tired that I never got around to it.

*

"Hey, you've reached the number that you've dialed; I'm not able to answer your call so leave your message." That was the answering machine to Jalissa's phone. For the past month I always received that answering machine. I was beginning to worry about her.

"Hey Lisa, this is Yesi. I'm calling to check up on you. This is bout the fourth time this month I've called you and got your voicemail. Call or write me and let me know that you're alright." With that message left I hung up. As many times as I called her this month and she hasn't responded back I don't think she listens to her voicemail. I don't even think she uses that phone anymore. Every time she calls she always calls from an *Unknown Caller* number.

"Yesi, you're needed to Mr. Landry room." I

turned around to see my co-worker Aja standing behind me looking at her chart.

"I just came from there," I said scrunching up my face.

"I don't know, he was hollering for you. What you do to that old man?"

"I ain't do nothing." I said as I walked away and headed to Mr. Landry room. As I walked down the hall I could hear Mr. Landry yelling and cursing whoever was in his room. When I walked in I had seen one of the new guys arguing with him.

"Mr. Landry what are you in here yelling for?" I said breaking in the middle of the two men.

"This man is trying to tell me that I can't have more than two visitor's a day. You always let me have three visitor's a day." He argued. I sighed. I looked towards the new guy who looked frustrated.

"I do allow him to have more than two visitor's a day." I then looked back at Mr. Landry. "But Mr. Landry you have to understand that he's not me and he may not allow you to do the things that I allow you to do."

"Well I don't want him as my caregiver."

"Well you're gonna have to take him because I'm going on vacation." I told him. "If you want someone else you have to take that up with Sherri." Mr. Landry just would not let it go so I excused myself and got the supervisor Sherri for him and clocked out so I could go home. I had better things to do than to sit and try to work visits out with him.

Malikaa

A million and one things were going through my mind as I sat across from my little sister. She looked so innocent sitting across from me with her young hands folded into her lap. Robyn looked up at me with confused eyes. I was just as confused as she was. I didn't know how to deal with a situation like this. Robyn was an honor roll student, on the volleyball team and a member of SGA. I just didn't understand how someone as smart as her could get pregnant at the age of fifteen. I know kids with her intelligence can get pregnant but I don't understand how my sister, my baby could do that, after hours of preaching to her about not having sex until she was well beyond ready.

"So what am I suppose to do?" she asked me with tears on the rim of her eye lids. I rubbed between my eyes; stress was not what I needed at the time.

"What do you think you should do Robyn?" Robyn shrugged her shoulders.

"I guess I'm suppose to get an abortion,"

"Is that what you want?" I asked her.

"I guess because I do want to finish school and go to college." She said as she made her career plans out in her head.

"Whatever you decide I'm here for you. I'm gonna let you sit and think about it and I'm going to go lay down cause chile' I need to after this." I told her. I walked down stairs and into the basement where my mom had finally turned it into an entertainment room after four years of dreaming about one. I flopped down on the couch and started flipping through the channels looking for anything that would hold my attention long enough for me to dose off.

I woke up to the sound of my phone ringing nonstop. I wasn't going to answer but the sound of Latoya Luckett's voice began to annoy me as her song *'Torn'* played over and over again. Reluctantly I answered the phone. Hopefully Darious would realize the sleepiness in my voice and decide to call me back. But I had seen that wouldn't happen once he continued on a conversation after my second time of telling him that I was asleep.

"What you tryna do this weekend?" Darious asked me.

"Well, it all depends on what Robyn decides

to do. I'm going to chill with her this weekend. We need some sisterly bonding."

"That's wassup. So when you gonna make some time for me?"

"I always make time for you. The question is when are you gonna make time for me. You always busy." I said to him.

"I'ma come past your place tonight. Make sure you be layin in the bed ready for me."

"Yeah, whateva," was what I told him. Though me and him have been talking for well over a year we had yet to have any type of sex, and lord knows I wanted to. He had this voice that made me want to come in my panties, and the way he holds me. I just melt in his big strong arms. As close as we came to getting down to the nitty gritty, I just couldn't see myself doing that to Rashaad. Rashaad and I had only been talking for two months when he was arrested for armed robbery. When I first met him it was love at first sight. I loved the way his dreads hung past his shoulders his caramel skin reminded me of a *payday*. His voice wasn't as deep as I would've like for it to be, so when I first met him he was kind of questionable.

"I love you."

"huh?"

"I said I love you." Darious repeated.

"I love you too." I said back. It was true. I was in love with two men at the same time. It was my fault; I shouldn't have allowed myself to get my feelings caught up.

"So look, I'm gonna come past your house around nine. Be home, not at your mom's house cause I'm not bout to be making that long as trip to pick you up."

I laughed, "Aight," we said our bye's and see you later and then hung up the phone.

*

I lay stretched out on my bed watching *Lifetime Movie Network.* As I was watching the movie *'Sleeping with the Enemy'* I wondered if something had happened with Lisa and what made her decided to leave; and if Yasmine was right, why she moved ten hours away from home. As I recall, she had her days just like everyone else when she felt down in the dumps; but like I said, who didn't? There was one day in particular that I do remember, it was Labor Day when she had a cookout at her house and I ended up staying the night at her house.

I had woken up to some loud yelling, I looked around the room and Lisa wasn't anywhere in there. I didn't want to get up and go out into the hallway to see what was going on so I stayed lying in the bed.

"You think you know shit! You don't know a damn thing! You so fuckin dumb." followed by, "You and your company can get the fuck up out my house!" rung out the loudest. The yelling and hollering went on for ten more minutes before I heard a loud bang against the wall. Moments later Lisa walked into the room with tears running down her face.

Yasmine called me around a quarter to six; her boys were loud in the background. That's how her house always was, never a quiet moment unless the boys were sleep or in school. Yasmine and I met through Lisa, in fact that's how we all met; Yasmine, Joi, and I. Instantly we clicked unlike me and Lisa. Even though I knew her longer, there was just something about her that threw me the wrong way. Maybe it was her sarcastic mouth, or the fact that she spoke whatever was on her mind and didn't care how it came out; whatever it was I just wasn't feeling it. Yasmine on the other hand was my girl, her and Joi.

"What you doing?" Yasmine asked me.

"Nothing, watching this movie on *Lifetime*." I told her stretching across my bed.

"Oh, girl these boys are drivin me crazy. I wish their dusty ass fava hurry up and come get them. Shit I need a break too."

"Um," was all I could say. I told her when she got pregnant with Josh not to have a baby by Robert cause he wasn't nothing but an around the way nigga and responsibility wasn't in his vocabulary. They had been together since our prom, and they have yet to settle down; seven years later, two children and still no ring; but always the same thing. 'I just gotta get my shit together. You know I love you and I wanna marry you.' I don't understand how she continuously put up with the bull. But hey, that's her life to live.

"I'm hungry, what you cookin?" I asked as my stomach growled.

"Nothin, I probably order some carryout since the boys gonna be gone."

"True, I don't have carryout money and I don't feel like cookin."

"Well I don't know what to tell you." She

told me. "Oh, I went out with that guy from the Poet Lounge."

"For real, where ya'll go?"

"Out to uh, damn what's the name of that place. It's on the tip of my tongue; Mike's or Michael's. You been there before?" She asked me.

"The teacher's store?" I asked confused.

"No girl, out to eat." I laughed.

"Oh, yeah me, Joi, Darell, and Darious went. I thought I told you about that."

"Naw you didn't. But it was nice. The food was okay, I don't think I'd go there again." I told her.

Jalissa

"So, you know you gotta take a drug test today right?" I said to the young man sitting across from me. He sat fondling with his hands as he shook his head. "Do you have the fifteen dollars to take the test?" He shook his head no. "Well, you can go ahead and take the test and when you come back next month you have to pay double. Understood?" The young man, who in the streets was known as Smoke, looked at me and nodded his head. His shoulder length dreads stood unorganized on top of his head. His smooth coffee brown skin hid the fact that he was in the peak of his puberty years. One couldn't tell that he was only fourteen. Within a week he went from five foot four to six feet. He was still in the stage where his voice was transitioning from a boy to a man.

I watched as the young man, whose government name is Randy, walk out of my office. The end of the day was nearing and I was so ready for it to be over. I looked into my desk drawer and took a glimpse at one of my cell phones. There were three missed calls with one voicemail. One call was from Malikaa, one was from Yesi, and the other was from an unknown number. Just as I was about to pick up the phone to call my home girl Angela, Randy walked back into the office. He sat and we, or shall I say I discussed his schooling situation. He knew that part of his probation was to continue to go to school, have clean urine, and to not hang around the same group of guys that he's been hanging around. Young men like him reminded me why I chose to do juvenile probation; so much potential, just guided by the wrong people.

I dragged my feet down to my building to see a group of young Hispanic boys. My neighborhood was field with Mexicans and Hispanics and just a few of us blacks and whites. It was like we were now considered the minorities. Well blacks have always been considered minorities but, they have now over powered us.

"Hola, Javio," I spoke to the one guy that I recognized. He lived across the hall from me with his mother and baby sister. I would watch him and his sister from time to time when their mother just wanted a break.

"Hola Senorita Lisa," he respectfully responded back. He was sitting in front of the building on his black and blue bike. "¿Brandon puede salir?" He asked referring to my three year old son Brandon. Living in a neighborhood filled with Spanish speaking people I had to learn the language. That was only way to survive. Plus it gave me advantage on picking up work. I smiled down at the boys as I made my way up the steps and to my apartment. From outside of the door I could hear the living room television on; it was blasting Cars. I could hear Lightning McQueen and Brandon saying, *"Turn right to go left! Guess what? I tried it, and you know what? This crazy thing happened - I went right!"* I opened the door to the house not to my liking. Brandon had toys scattered around on the living room floor. My boy friend Cory shoes laid in the middle of the dining room, his coat was thrown on the couch. The trash had yet to be taken out, and I told him to get on that when I left out this morning. Dishes were still in the sink; but the only thing done was that the dinner was cooked. I could deal with Brandon's mess because that was my child. I expected to clean up after him.

"Hey ma," I smiled down at my big boy. He looked so much like his daddy that it sickened me. He was an unexpected pregnancy, just when I thought I was getting out of that toxic relationship, and I thought I was getting away scott free I find out I was pregnant. I was at work when I had actually passed out. I thought it was just from exhaustion, but no, they had done some test on me and the doctor came back with a wide smile on his face telling me that I was pregnant. When they did the sonogram it showed that I was four months pregnant. Brandon came two months early, I assume from my lack of care during my early trimester. Other than being premature he came out with asthma; but *other* than that, my baby is healthy. I couldn't imagine my life without him now.

"Hey baby, how was school?" I asked. He shrugged his shoulders, still into the movie. "Spell 'he'." I instructed. Education was very important to me, so every chance I had gotten I instilled knowledge into his young mind and quizzed him on it.

"h-e," he quickly said. "Ma, be quiet, I want to watch Cars." I laughed. *Cars* was by far one of his favorite movie. I found that interesting, because I had gotten the movie for my god-son Xavier when he was around Brandon's age and he too loved that movie.

I left Brandon to his movie and walked into my bedroom to see Cory stretched out across the bed yappin his gums on the phone. I watched as he extended his average limbs across the bed. Once he noticed that I was standing in the doorway with my hands placed impatiently on my hips he hoped off of the bed and made his way to me.

"Why the hell does my hou—" he cut me off by place one of his fingers over my lips as if to tell me to be quiet. From my lips he moved his hands down to the curve of my hips. He leaned in to give me a kiss but I pulled away from him. "What the fuck, don't shush me. Why the hell does my house look like this Cory?" He sucked his teeth and stepped away from me. His conversation continued on the phone. Each second he ignored me my frustration level was shooting to the roof. "Ugh!" I blew, trying to get some of my frustration out. Cory attempted to rub my arm trying to calm me down, I snatched back.

"No, console that bitch you talkin to," I snapped before exiting to the living room to clean up the mess.

I didn't *know* if Cory was actually talking to a female; but I *knew* he was. Did that make sense? It wouldn't be the first time he sat in my face and talked to other females. Though I didn't approve of it, I just couldn't bring myself to say anything. I liked the fact that our relationship was almost conflict free. I left him alone most of the time, just tried to encourage him every so often to get up and get a job. I couldn't survive off of my income alone; paying rent, utilities, and cable and feeding myself, a child and a grown ass man just wasn't going to work. I only kept him around because I didn't want to be alone. We never went out and communication was shot, the only thing that was still good was the sex. And that was a sometimes.

I'd left my home three years ago. I had just packed up all of my things and left, and I didn't plan on turning around to cry for the past that I had left behind. The constant fighting that was happening between Brandon's dad and I; and I mean *fighting*. I got tired of covering up black eyes and bruised limbs. So, I packed all of my things with my hopes and dreams and moved up north; praying that the Lord would see me through. I cried my whole way up to Chicago.

"Awe shit, don't come at me with that," Cory said. I just stared blankly at him. The more I looked at him the more I kept thinking, *'what the hell am I doing?'* I deserved much more than what he was bringing into me, and hell, he was bringing me nothing. I wanted more, I deserved more, and I was going to get more.

"That's just nasty. I wish Darrell would sleep with one of my sisters. I would turn into Lorena Bobbitt on him." I thought out loud as I watched a repeat of the Maury Provach show. It was Veterans' Day and I took that opportunity to lounge around the house and hopefully get some quality time with my husband while Camille was at my moms' house. I glanced over at the clock resting on the night stand. It was still very early in the morning. I managed to pull myself out of bed and over to the window to see that Darrell's car was still parked out front.

It had been over a year since I had cooked breakfast for the both of us. We had always been on the go, so much in a hurry. Since I was home I figured it wouldn't hurt for the both of us to sit at the table and eat together. I was halfway in the middle of finishing up breakfast when Darrell walked into the kitchen and over to the stove where I was standing. He was so close that I could feel his breath on the nape of my neck. His natural scent was intoxicating. I took a deep breath being turned on every second that he stood behind me.

"What you cooking?" Darrell asked me as he scanned the island. I placed a smirk on my face.

"Just some breakfast; you going to eat with me?"

"Um, yeah, I think I have time." A smile spread across my face as I began to prepare our plates. We sat at the dining room table having small talk and eating our breakfast. Our conversation seemed forced, neither one of us seemed to know what really to talk about. I watched him as he slid his plate to the side and began reading the *Metro* section of the Washington Post. My sexual build up took over my entire body. I was always sexually attracted to Darrell, that's what I use to like most about our relationship. I eased my way behind him and began to nibble at his ear. I felt him inhale, I knew his spots. I took my hand and rubbed it down his chest and continued to nibble. I knew just what to do to drive him to rip my clothes off. At least I thought I did.

"Come on Joi, what are you doing?" he asked me.

"Nothing, just enjoying the moment that we're having right now." I moved in front of him and hopped my ass on the table.

"I don't have time for that right now,"

"Baby, I know you have a couple of hours to spare." My legs were flying eagle. I pulled him towards me, in between my warmth. I looked him in his brown eyes and seen sympathy replaced with guilt. I knew he was cheating on me. I knew there was someone else pleasing my man. I just didn't want to believe it. I didn't want to believe that someone was ripping my *happy* family apart. I leaned in for a kiss, but he pulled away. My heart fell to the pit of my stomach. We hadn't had sex in eight months. He hadn't touched me in six months. I was sexually deprived and frustrated. He left my coochie wetter than the Atlantic Ocean, yet it had more cob webs than an abandoned house.

"Joi, I don't have time for this," he said. "I gotta get ready to go to the office." On a day when all office buildings are closed, he wants to go into the office. He grabbed my face and gave me a kiss on the forehead. My blood boiled. A forehead kiss, really? After years of marriage all I add up to is a forehead kiss. I inhaled deeply, suffocating all the tears that tried to make themselves known. I watched as he walked away from me and disappeared into the living room.

"Oh, and don't wait up for me tonight; I'm

going to be working late in the office." I hopped off of the counter. "He's a damn lie; I know a cheatin nigga when I see one." I mumbled to myself as I walked upstairs.

Malikaa

"Marrissa, why is your voice the first thing I hear when I get out of my car, a block away." I said as soon as I swung the door open. All eyes fell on me, and the ones who weren't able to turn around stretched their eyes far as they would go.

"Nu uh bitch, don't come in here and try to run shit," Marrissa said. Her burgundy tipped locks pulled back into a ponytail exposing her coffee brown face.

"I know right, where the fuck you been at?" Nicolas asked. Nicolas was the salon's 'Queen'. Not a day when he was not on his *diva* status. You would either love him or hate him.

"Don't try and come for me, and it's none of ya'll business where I been." I said dropping my things down at my station. Joi was already sitting in my chair. I was running late for her appointment. Darious had me out all night. I hope she didn't have anything planned. I ran my hand across my forehead. I hated the heat. You could just get out of the shower and still feel dirty because of the humidity.

"Hey Joi, you got something planned today?" I asked.

"No, I'm just gonna stop by Darrell's office later today." I frowned my eyebrows at her. Something was up. She didn't usually go up to his job unless it was a dire emergency, and she nor Camille was hurt so I wanted to know what was up.

"You know what, I'm going to wash my face off then I'ma come and dig all in your stuff." Joi laughed.

When I came back from the bathroom Nicolas was in the middle of the floor trying to follow the video. I smiled and shook my head at his nonsense.

"I thought this was a place of business," I asked out loud. Nicolas stopped in his tracks and dramatically swung his head around towards me.

"Ooooh, you a party pooper!"

"Let me be; if Mrs. Douglas was here, you wouldn't be all over the place like that." Nicolas rolled his eyes at me.

"Sorry ya'll, we gotta go back to whispering and singing old negro spirituals. But don't sing them too loud cause the warden don't want us to have any type of fun." I rolled my eyes at him.

"Ya'll dumb," Marissa chuckled.

"Yeah, whateva. Ain't nobody say you can't have any fun, but all that jumpin around and stuff, cut it out." You could hear the older ladies in the salon agreeing with me. I ran my hands through Joi's matted hair. "Damn, did you wash this stuff?"

"Yeah," she giggled.

"Well, did you comb it?"

"Yeah, you know this stuff is thick!" she explained. I laughed. Her hair needed a miracle; I don't think my comb would make it through it.

"What am I doin to this stuff?" she took a deep breath.

"Just cut it all off," I stopped combing her hair and looked at her through the mirror. "What?" she asked me.

"Why you cutting your hair? I'll make you a wig so it seems like your hair is short,"

"No, I want my hair. This thick stuff on my head cut off! Do you want me to start it off for you?" a look of seriousness was written on her face.

"You must want Darrell to kill me." She rolled her eyes at the mention of his name, but I kept going. "I'm not cutting your hair, besides you *KNOW* I don't know how to cut no hair. I do wigs, and tracks."

"Screw Darrell," My eyes bulged out of my head. When did the *'I love that man,'* turn into *'Screw that man.'*

"What's wrong? Just two weeks ago you were screaming about how much you loved your husband."

"Well my *husband* is cheating on me," she pouted. My mouth dropped open.

"With who?"

"I donno."

"Well, how do you know Joi?" I asked. I didn't want her jumping into conclusions and ruining their marriage.

"I just know. For a month now he has cancelled on our lunch dates. He comes home around one, two am. And—" she sighed deeply. "We haven't had sex in almost a year, probably longer."

"Well got damn, a year?" I was shocked. Joi

always bragged about how good Darrell had did her, or was doing her.

"Yes girl, and shoot, batteries are expensive!" I burst into laughter. She giggled.

"I'm going to pop up at his job, if he's really working."

"You know I love you, but I really think that is a bad idea." She sucked her teeth.

"Why?"

"Because, if you go searching for something, don't be mad when you finally find it."

"Well, if I don't go searching then I'll never find; which means I'll never know what's going on. And that will leave me looking like an ass." I just left it at that. I didn't want to continue to go back and forth with her over something she thought was apparently right. I just hope at the end of the day I wouldn't have to be fighting back an *'I told you so.'*

Yasmine

"Come on now, what the frick!" I said pushing my freshly manicured nails to hit the ignore button on my cell. The guy that I had met a month ago kept calling my phone. I told him after two weeks of talking to him that I thought it was best that we didn't talk anymore. He was trying to rush us into being in a relationship. Always said that I was his girl friend, and then tried to tell me where I could go. I was not having that. I was so glad that he had not known where I lived. He just didn't get it cause he continued to call me every day, all day.

"Who is that?" Robert asked while attiring in his sleep. I shook my head before answering him.

"No one, important anyways." I told him, popping a Goober in my mouth. I sat up for two hours watching repeats of 'Keeping up with the Kardashians' and going through two boxes of Goobers. A heating pad rested on my pelvic area. I hated being female one week out of every month.

Time was moving extremely slow that day. It felt like it had been two in the afternoon for the past three hours. Robert lay beside me sleeping like he worked a full time job and the boys were outside playing. Any other time I would have loved the peace and quiet but today, quietness was my worst enemy. I glanced at the clock that read two forty-five and debated on if I wanted to call Lisa for the hundredth time. Or see if Malikaa or Joi was doing anything. I wanted to call Joi and see what was going on with her and Darrell. Malikaa called me and gave me the 411 on the situation. I wouldn't be surprised if he was cheating on her. Every since our friend, Rose seen him kissing on someone else that wasn't Joi, he had rubbed me the wrong way. I wonder what Lisa would say if she knew what was going on.

Now, Lisa never liked Darrell as long as I could remember. She tolerated him because that's who her best friend fell in love with. But from what she has told me, she could see past this demeanor he possessed and the sad, pity party stories Joi told her about his past. I was always strict on the saying, *'never let a man come in between your friendship; because he'll be gone in the wind your friends would still be here.'* But in their case, that was not cutting it. A man had come through and decapitated their friendship.

Just as I was about to pick up my phone to call Joi, Roberts phone started going off. I looked at him and then at his phone. I picked his phone up and hesitated on answering it. I wasn't going to until I seen Erica's name and picture popped up on the screen. I got up off of the couch and walked into the back room before answering.

"Hello," I spoke into the phone.

"Hello, who is this?" Erica asked. The sound of her high pitched voice boiled my soul. She was the reason Robert and I didn't work out. I would love to say he downgraded to some ugly girl, but it was just that. She wasn't ugly. It angered me because someone as pretty as her didn't deserve to be with someone like Robert; just as well as I didn't. Erica was a red bone, damn near white; five-six with long toned legs.

"Does it matter who it is?" I asked her with just as much attitude that she was giving me. She sucked her teeth.

"Put Rob on the phone." I hung up on her. Didn't think twice. Seconds later his phone began to ring again. It was Erica. I answered on the first ring.

"Little girl, could you please stop calling this phone?" Little girl was exactly what she was. Erica was a seventeen year old high school dropout who spent her days with Robert smoking and God knows what else.

'This aint yo' phone, so im gonna keep callin until you give him the damn phone." Her immaturity was showing. My patients were wearing thin.

"I'm asking—no, I'm telling you nicely. Please stop calling this phone." There was shuffling on the other end. I could imagine her face turning fire engine red and her eyes doing a three-sixty.

"These bitches keep testing me," was the last thing I heard before the phone grew quiet. I pulled the phone away from my ear and looked at it. She had hung up on me. I walked back into the living room and eased the phone back on the table without him even knowing that it was gone.

Yasmine

"Why you answerin my phone Yasmine?" Robert yelled through the phone. I pulled the phone away from my ear and looked at it as if it had three screens. I could still hear him ranting about something that I had no clue as to what he was talking about. His attitude was starting to ruin mines.

"What are you talkin about Rob?" I was trying my hardest to speak in a nice and calm tone. After all, I was at work.

"So now you gonna act like you don't know what the fuck I'm talkin bout Yesi?" I looked around to see if there was anyone around. The area was clear.

"Who you getting an attitude with? I don't have time to be sitting here arguing with you,"

"Why you tellin people not to call my phone? I don't do that to yours." He said to me.

"Who are you talkin bout? Who did I tell not to call your phone?" I knew damn well who he was talking about. He hesitated before saying Erica's name. He was angry as if I cared.

"If ya'll not together why should it matter if I told her not to call your phone anymore?" He didn't say anything.

"That's not the point Yasmine, don't answer my fuckin phone anymore."

"Robert, I don't have time for you, these kids that you mess with or anything else. Don't call me off some bullshit, I'm at work and got stuff to do. I might call you when I get home." I told him before I left him to sit listening to the silence on the other end of the phone.

Malikaa

"You have a prepaid call. You will not be charged for this call. This call is from-Rashaad Blake-," The voice recorder spoke into the phone. I pushed five until I could hear Rashad on the other end of the phone saying 'hello'.

"Hey baby, how feelin today?" I asked. I was always concerned about him. Jail was a world of its own, so I was afraid that he was getting sucked into that world and never coming out.

"Wassup babe, I'm good. Missin yo' ass." I smiled. "Countin down the days until we see each other."

"Me too baby. Five more months, not much longer." It was hard communicating with a lover through a telephone call once a week. Sometimes every two weeks. But when Rashad calls we would just talk as if he was still out. The hardest part was the end of the fifteen minute long conversation. Sometimes we would have time to say everything we wanted to say. And there are other times when we are right in the middle of saying *'I love you'* when the phone cuts off.

Our fifteen minute phone calls go by so fast. It seems as if we had just gotten on the phone when we were saying our good-byes. I continued cleaning up with Rashad on my mind. I couldn't wait until he got home. His lips against mines, our bodies intertwined. Umm…I knew exactly what Joi was saying about batteries not being cheap. I was sitting right in her boat, except I actually had a man who wanted me; he was just unavailable at the moment. And although I had Darious to keep me company, Rashad is where my commitment lies.

Rashad and I spoke on numerous occasions about the family we planned to start once he got out. Little Britney and Michael is what we planned to name our children if we were to have a boy and a girl. Once he got on his feet we were going to move probably into Virginia or further out in Maryland. I was more than excited to start my family.

*

'What Band' interrupted my T.V. show. I contemplated on answering but I knew that if I didn't, she was going to call back.

"Hey Nakia," I adjusted myself back into my comfortable position on the couch. Feet under my butt, body under my royal purple throw blanket and phone resting between my shoulder and cheek.

"Wassup Meme? What you doin?" Her words dragged. Nakia had this exaggerated way of talking when she was in the mist of trying to work out a favor from someone. I exhaled a deep breath that I had no idea that I was holding in. I concentrated on the t.v. for a few seconds, trying to hear what they were saying.

"Nothin, I'm all into this movie on *LMN*. What you up to?" I wasn't really interested in what she was doing, but I was trying to get to the point. I really wanted to get back to this movie Jennifer Love Hewitt stared in, sleeping with all the high rolling men for money.

"Nothin, me and Frank bout to go out to eat," it's coming. I know it is.

"That's waasup, where ya'll goin?"

"Girl, I don't know. He wanna try and do the surprise shit." All I could say was *'oh'* "I need a favor though," There it go.

"What?" a slight irritation could be heard in my voice.

"I need you to make me a wig."

"I just made you one Nakia," I whined.

"I know, but we're going out and I want something different. And since you make them sooooooo good." I rolled my eyes as far as they would go in the back of my head. My line beeped. I looked at the phone and seen that it was Joi calling in. I was waiting for three days to hear from her. I needed to know what happened when she went down to Darrell's office.

"Aw man, Nakia, somebody's on my other line. Bring the hair up here cause I really gotta take the call." I said trying to rush her off of the phone. I at least waited until she said *okay* before I clicked over on her.

"Hello?" I spoke.

"Hey Malikaa, what you doing?" she spoke dryly.

"I was watching t.v. but Nakia just called and asked me to make a wig for her. So now I'm sitting here waiting for her to get here.

"Oh, okay; I was going to ride over there. But I don't even feel like it now." I nodded my head as if she could see me.

"You suck," I simply stated. "Buuuuuuut, enough of me trying to wait until you say something. What happened when you went down to Darrell's job?"

"Girl," I could imagine her rolling her big brown eyes. "So, yesterday I finally had the chance to go down to his office. When I got there, his secretary gave me this strange look and she was all nervous. I just nicely looked at her and asked for him. She said he was at a lunch meeting."

"Well, maybe he was at a meeting." I told her.

"Yeah, I guess. But I didn't mention anything to him about going to his job."

"Joi, you got a descent man; stop trying to find things wrong with him. That's the fastest way to ruin your marriage."

"I guess you're right," the phone went silent for a minute. I just let her gather her thoughts as I went back into the movie. "Malikaa, I'm gonna call you back, I think Darrell just came home. Camille and I may swing by there later." We said our good-byes and ended our call.

I walked downstairs to see Darrell helping Camille out of her shoes. Shoes always come off at the front door. I don't play the shoes in the house. Light carpet is hard to clean and once it gets dirty it looks like the whole room is dirty. I always wanted a house with wall to wall carpet, white or egg shell. It made a room look bigger than what it really was, and more elegant. As I looked at the way they interacted, Camille and her dad, I couldn't suppress the smile on my face. Maybe I was *trying* to find something wrong with Darrell, when there was nothing wrong. He was just at the point where he had to *really* focus on the cases he had coming in. Camille was the first one to notice me standing on the stairs.

"Hey mommy," she shrieked. She was a dramatic child; loved being the center of attention. I wanted to start trying to put her in some commercials but Darrell refused to exploit his little princess. *"Wait until she gets older. I want her to enjoy her childhood."* He would tell me.

"Hey baby, you have fun at grandma house?" I asked her. She nodded her head. I walked all the way down the stairs until I stood just inches away from my husband. "Hey baby," I wanted to kiss him. I wanted to feel his lips against mine. I wanted to see if that spark was still there. But I didn't.

"Hey," he simply said. I folded my arms over my chest and walked into the living room, following after Camille. She turned to look at me as I came in the room. She was over by the DVDs.

"I want to watch Tinkerbell."

"Joi, come here," Darrell called. I put the movie on for her before I went looking for him. He was in his office. I leaned my body on the door frame. He looked up from his computer.

"Why you standing in the door way?" he asked. I wasn't sure how to answer him because what I wanted to say was going to come out as if I had an attitude and I wasn't trying to start anything. I just shrugged my shoulders.

"What did you call me for?"

"Come here," I reluctantly walked over to him. I stood directly in front of his desk. A few seconds passed before he took his eyes off of his laptop and looked at me. His hands folded under his chin, elbows resting on the counter. My hands rested on my hips. My eyes roamed around the room. It had been awhile since I was in his office. His office looked like the average office of a lawyer. His furniture was either black or cherry oak wood. On one side of his office he had a bookshelf filled with law books, psychology books, and a few books that had nothing to do with his career. On the other side of his office sat a black leather love seat; hanging over top of it a picture of Malcolm X was place. The inscription under the picture where his fingers were resting against his head read: *"The future belongs to those who prepare for it today."*

I use to love coming into his office when he was working long hours at work. His scent wrapped around the stitching of the couch.

"I'm having dinner guest tonight," I arched an eyebrow. I didn't plan on cooking, I didn't feel like cooking. I was just going to order a pizza or maybe Chinese.

"When were you going to tell me this?" I asked. Now it was evident that I had a slight attitude. His body slouched back in his chair. His hands placed firmly on the arms of the chair.

"Today, right now," I drew my head back. It had to register to me how he had just talked to me.

Talking to me like I was dumb. Like I was one of his clients.

"Excuse me?" I had to make sure I heard him right. He had the same amount of sass in his voice as he did the first time. "D, I didn't plan on cooking tonight. Can't you reschedule?"

"No, just whip something up." He kissed me on my cheek before walking out of the office. Aggravation wasn't even close to what I was feeling.

I managed to create a dinner out of spaghetti and garlic bread. It was far from what I had a taste for but I was not in the mood to make this lavish dinner for his guest. I sat across from a petite woman with an ample amount of make-up decorated her butter pecan complexion; jet black tracks shaped her oval face. I could not lie, she was gorgeous. I watched as she laughed one of those perfect cutesy laughs. My eyes glazed over her perfectly manicured nails, her lips curved perfectly into a smile. Everything about that woman was perfect. It was a relief when I had seen her come through the door with a date. Patrick was his name I believed. She introduced him as her boyfriend, but he had one too many cups of sugar in his coffee; he was a very metro-sexual type of guy. He wore dark denim fitted jeans, a white shirt with a cardigan to cover it. His lips were greasier than KFC's chicken.

I sat opposite of Darrell's company playing in my food. I wasn't hungry; I didn't even feel like being bothered with anyone. I was pretty upset that Darrell invited people over without clearing anything over with me. I was zoning in and out of their conversation just in case they asked me about whatever it was that they were talking about, I'd know the just of it. I watched the interaction between him and the girl Stephanie. I had seen the sparkle in her eye as she looked at him. Darrell was a big flirt, and though it was not with words, he was flirting with her big time. Eye fucking the shit out of her. I looked over to Patrick to see if he was seeing what my eyes were seeing; he didn't. He laughed with them, and engaged in every ounce of their conversation. I felt myself growing so impatient with the whole dinner with those people. I so badly wanted to ask 21 questions, but right then wasn't really the time; not with Camille sitting right beside me. I looked over at Camille as she picked in her food and pretended to be feeding her doll.

"Jay baby, you okay?" I heard Darrell say. I turned to face him. I tried to soften my face, but I knew it wasn't working.

"Yeah, why you ask?" I said picking my fork up and twirling it around on my plate. He shook his head, giving me this look he always did when I was embarrassing him in front of *'important'* people. I just rolled my eyes at him.

"So Joi, I hear that you're a writer." Stephanie said as she prop her elbows on the table and rested her head onto her hands.

"Oh, so you've heard about me?" I said as I looked over at my husband. "That I am. I own my own publishing company." I told her proudly. "And I'm sorry, what is it that you do?" I said with much sarcasm in my voice. I didn't mean to come off as if I was belittling her, but it just happened to roll off of my tongue that way. She smiled a bright smile. Her teeth were perfect.

"At the moment, I'm interning for Darrell. I'm in my last year at Howard." I nodded my head, followed by a sarcastic laugh.

"First name basis with your boss, I wish I had that privilege when I was working under someone." I stated.

"Joi, stop it." Darrell said. I looked at him, his glare was like death.

"Stop what Darrell? I'm just making conversation,"

"Mommy can I get ice cream?" I heard Camille say. I looked over at her; she still had most of her food on her plate.

"No Camille, you haven't eaten any of your

food." she pouted.

"But I don't want it." she whined.

"And you don't want ice cream either. And stop that whining." I told her.

"Take a few more bites and daddy will get you some ice cream." I watched as her little eyes light up. I chuckled and shook my head. He always did that. I tell her no and he undermines my authority. I was trying my best not to bring our family business out while his company was there. They continued to carry on a conversation. I completely zoned them out. I was beyond ready for them to leave. I didn't want to be rude and leave the table so I sat there blankly staring into space.

Jalissa

I sat at on the bench with my friend Sierra as we watched our children on the playground. Occasionally we had to get up and guide them on the slide or push them on the swing. It was a nice and hot, with a slight breeze in Chicago that day. I had so much on my mind that I just needed time to clear it. Sierra was the first person I met when I moved up north. I was the new girl in the office, and everyone could tell. I'm naturally a quiet person in foreign situations, so for a couple of months I was to myself; then one day this petite white girl with fire engine red hair came and started a conversation with me. The conversation was as small as, "Where you from?" from there we would speak when we seen each other, then we'd start taking our lunches together; that soon graduated to hanging out outside of work.

"I'm bout to leave Corey's dingy ass alone. Every time I go in that damn house it smells like feet and sweaty balls." I frowned as I spoke. Sierra laughed.

"Feet and sweaty balls though," I giggled.

"I'm serious though. His ass is getting on my

nerves, and his red ass won't go and get a damn job. I asked him to watch Brandon while I go to work one Saturday, you know this nigga gonna catch an attitude." I turned my whole body to look at her before speaking again. "I know that ain't your child, but you ain't bout to be layin up in my got damn house just eatin up my shit and not contributing to anything. You bout to pitch in and do something."

"I don't know why you ain't been leave his ass. I knew from the first time I seen him that he wasn't shit." I shook my head. Yeah, I knew I was a dumb one; just hoping and praying that a nigga was gonna change. I turned back around towards the playground and crossed my legs at the ankles.

"Dick was just good, that's why my dumb ass still with him. But shit, good dick only gets you but so far." Sierra laughed while I sighed. "Bitch gotta go though."

"True…" it was silent between the two of us for a minute before Sierra spoke again. "Girl, tell me why Kevin came to my house last night, after being missin for a week." She told me. I don't know what was wrong with us females these days, always putting up with niggas shit, over and over again.

"Umm, you took his ass back in didn't you?" I asked.

"Fuck no. Michelle was ova anyway, I told him I had company and he had to go. Maybe I'll talk to him tomorrow." Sierra liked to dip and dabble on both sides of the team. I learned one thing about Sierra dating rituals. She liked her men black and built. Not Vin Deziel built, just a little athletic. She liked her women white and petite like her. They had to be girly girl.

"I don't like a butch. If I wanted a man, I'll go and date a man." She told me one day during one of our drunken nights. There were a couple times when she tried to her hand with me, but I was not having it; no part of me was interested in putting my mouth on her 'love box.' Kevin and Sierra had been in an on and off again relationship long before I had moved up north. She reminded me so much of Yasmine, the way she handles her relationship with her baby father; knowing that he doing all the dirt in the world but still fold under his touch.

We sat at the playground until the sun was beginning to go down; I needed Brandon to be good and sleepy by time we got back home. He was going to eat, I was gonna wash him down and he would be ready to close those big beautiful eyes of his. By time we had gotten home it was a quarter to nine. I hadn't intended on staying out so late, I had wanted to stay up for a while to get some work done before I called it a night; but that clearly was not about to happen. I was tired myself.

When I pulled up to my neighborhood I seen Corey sitting outside on the hood of his car talking on his cell phone. I rolled my eyes as I pulled into my parking spot in front of my building. As I got out of my car I had seen a group of young men that hung out in front of my building. They weren't any trouble, so I didn't care much about them loitering. I opened the back door to pull Brandon out of his car seat before locking up my 2006 Honda Accord.

"Hola Senorita," I smiled up at the young men as I adjusted Brandon in my arms, in the process I dropped my keys. One of the young men bent down to retrieve my dropped item.

"Gracias," I told them before walking into my building and up the one flight of steps to my home. I didn't even bother to lock the door because like clockwork Corey was coming into the house. My mind was doing wonders as I prepared Brandon for bed. That night I was finally going to listen to the little person inside of me. Once I had gotten out of the shower, I walked ass naked into my room and fucked Corey like I had never fucked him before. I wanted him to know what he was going to be missing out on.

We lay drenched in each other's sweat, entangled in my blue sheets. I was trying to figure out in my head how to tell him that he had to go. What we once shared was now over and it was time for him to get off of the train. "Corey," I said. I knew he was on his way to sleep, that was his thing; bust a nut then roll over. "Corey," I said louder.

"Hmm?" He said, eyes still closed, making himself comfortable in my bed.

"This is your last night here; this is was your last night dippin into my 'love box'. Tomorrow, I want you out of my house. You and everything you own."

Malikaa

"What the fuck, go! The damn ambulance is on the otha side of the street!" I screamed. Darious looked at me for my outburst. I was an aggressive passenger side driver. I would admit that I was one of those people that processed not one single form of a driver's license but wanted to tell everyone else how to drive.

"What the hell is wrong with you?" he asked me. I rolled my eyes at him.

"I'm annoyed, these non-drivers." I looked out the window with a scowl on my face.

"You do know you're suppose to pull over regardless of the side the ambulance or police is on." He informed me. I sucked my teeth and rolled my eyes. My lack of knowledge for the road was quite embarrassing.

"Well, the emergency isn't on this side, so I don't see the point in us pulling over." I was in the middle of my crucial irritable moments. Everything and everyone was annoying me. It was hot outside and that made my irritability level sky rocket. We were headed to a cookout one of his aunt's house; they were having one of those end of the season cookouts. I was a nervous wreck because I had never met any of his family before. Well no one besides Jalissa. My mind was telling me that we were moving too fast. Darious was just supposed to be someone who kept me busy until Rashaad got out. I felt my heart longing for Darious every time we were away from each other, but when Rashaad called I'm like "Darious who?"

His aunt's house was packed with people. She lived in a residential town home area with assigned parking spaces, so it took us a good minute to find some place to park. When we walked up to the town home there were people sitting on the front lawn playing cards, and smoking cigarettes.

"Aye, Dee here!" One of the guys yelled with a cigarette in one hand and his cards in another. The smoke from his cigarette drifted into his face.

"Wassup Dee," another card player said. There were four players sitting at the small card table, so I would assume that a spades game was in play. Two males and two females occupied the chairs while three other people stood around. Darious went over to one of the men, the older one that he resembled, and embraced him in one of those manly hugs and then he went to the older woman and kissed her on the cheek.

"Hey ma," he said.

"Hey baby," she said. My stomach did summersaults. "Who's this?" she asked.

"Oh, this my girlfriend Malikaa," I smiled. *Girlfriend?* Yeah things were defiantly becoming too serious too soon. "Malikaa this my muva and fava," he introduced us.

"Hello," I said as I gave a small wave.

"Hey honey, you ain't gotta be actin all shy. We ain't gonna talk about you when you leave." His dad said.

"I know, we'll do it while you here." A female said as she looked up from her cards and at the four of us. Everyone started laughing. I smirked because I didn't find anything funny.

"Deanna shut up," Darrell said. I was assuming Deanna was his sister because she too resembled his father. All three of them dark brown tone, hefty, dark orbs, and all sported a low cut fade. Deanna wasn't your average woman; she dressed the part of a guy. My suspicions were right when a beautiful light skinned voluptuous woman walked out of the house and over to Deanna with a beautiful little boy in her arms. She leaned down and kissed her on the lips as she placed the little boys in her arms.

"Hey Dee," the voluptuous woman said to Darious.

"Hey Payton," Darious spoke.
"This your girl?" she asked as she looked at me.

"Yeah, Malikaa this Payton," I smiled at her.

"Hey," she said.

"Well go introduce your girlfriend to your grandmother. She in the house," his mom told him. He grabbed my hand and led me into the dimly lit house. The house was lit with only the sunlight piercing through the outdated curtains. There were a lot of people in the house; everyone was packed in there like a can of sardines. I believed I met everyone in his family that day. Everywhere I turned someone was asking me who I was, giving me a hug, saying hello.

We pulled up to my house a quarter past ten. I had fun at his family cookout. I hadn't laughed so hard in God knows how long. It was refreshing to be around a family that could joke around about anything and not take everything so serious. I was tired but I wasn't sleepy; I just wanted to lay stretched out across my bed and watch T.V. I didn't protest when Darious got out of the car and followed me into my apartment. I also didn't back down when he left butterfly kisses along the nape of my neck. The only reaction he got out of me was the moistness from between my legs. I was now saying *'Rashaad who?'* as pieces of my clothes left my body. Every part of my body that his rough manly hands hand touched felt like lightning bolts pulsating through my body. So protesting, fighting back or arguing were discarded from my vocabulary as he laid me on my bed, tongues clashing against each other like waves on a sea shore. It had been over a year since I felt any type of penetration between my legs other than a plastic toy that stuck to the wall of my shower. So I lie on my back and let him explore me.

Jalissa

I sat at my desk devastated at the news that I had just heard. I couldn't move, I couldn't cry, scream or get mad; I was numb. I knew it was coming but I didn't expect for it to be so soon. I had this weird feeling in the pit of my stomach when I woke that morning, so I had a feeling that something bad was going to happen that day. I was in the middle of sorting papers on my desk when my phone just kept going off. It just kept ringing over and over again. My heart sunk to the pit of my stomach when I seen a number that I had recognized but I didn't have them stored in my phone and I knew that didn't have my number because I never called them. *How the hell he get my number?* Again my phone wrung. I decided to answer because if he found a way to get my number after years of no contact and he kept calling me back to back, I knew something had to be wrong.

"Um, hello?" I said into the phone.

"Jalissa, we been tryna call you all day," I heard my brother say with so much sadness into the phone.

"How did you get my number?" I was curious to know, although I knew it was no one but

Yasmine who gave it up, but why?

"Granddaddy died this morning." He ignored my question and gave me the worst feeling that my heart has ever felt.

"What?" I heard my brother sobbing on the other end. I could picture the tears running down his face as he had to break the news to me. I knew it was tarring him up because they were so close; my grandparents practically raised my brother seeing that my mom was in the prime of her teen years when she had him.

"Granddaddy died, you gotta come home." He told me. Just hearing those words made my heart turn in knots. He hadn't met Brandon yet, he couldn't go. I sighed deeply not wanting my ears to believe the words that were being told to me.

"I'll be there," I told him before hanging up, not allowing him to say anything else. I had to prepare myself mentally to go back down to Maryland. I placed my phone on my desk and laid back into my chair closing my eyes. Unknowingly tears ran down my face.

I waited until my lunch time before going into my supervisor's office. I tried so hard to keep my composure until my grandpa and died fell in the same sentence. I was able to get out of work and attend my granddad's funeral. I had a week to go to

Maryland and watch life; lies and secrets unfold before my eyes.

I walked inside of my apartment ready to fall out. I had a headache from crying my whole way home, not to mention the ongoing ringing of my phone. Corey was calling me back to back; he had been calling me since the day after I kicked him out. He tried to come back to my house two days later, but I had gotten my locks changed. He thought I was playing, but no, I was dead ass serious. I already had a child; I didn't need to be taking care of someone else's. Before I allowed my body to fall restlessly on my bed I decided that it was best that I got our things together before it was time for me to pick Brandon up; because I knew when he gets home I wouldn't be able to do anything with him being all over the place, pulling all of his toys out on the floor. I was still trying to figure out why he has to pull *all* his toys out when he's only going to play with is one or two of them. It took me almost an hour to pack a week worth of clothes. Once finished I called up Sierra to make sure she would look after my place while I was gone.

"Yeah girl, I'll stop by when I get off of work to make sure everything is okay." Sierra said.

"Okay good cause I don't trust Corey's ass." I

said while rolling my eyes as if she could see me. she laughed. "I'm serious. His red ass just keeps callin my fuckin phone."

"Are you serious?"

> "Yeah girl. I told you he tried to come back but I had already changed the locks."

"And you want my boney ass to guard your house?" I laughed.

"His ass not gonna show up. Just make sure no one break into my shit please."

"Aight hun," I was satisfied with her answer. I knew that I had to get Brandon in a few, get him nice and tired with the park because I planned to make that eight hour trip to the DMV in the morning and I needed him well rested.

It was hard waking up first thing in the morning, having to get myself ready as well as a small child; especially when that child was not a morning person. A trait he inherited from his dad. Kicking, screaming, and dragging his but made me want to knock him up aside his head; especially days when I was running late. It took all of two hours to get the both of us ready. I was thirty minutes behind schedule and Brandon was still dragging around.

"Brandon, bring your ass on and get in the car." I shouted at him, now frustrated.

"Lisa! Lisa!" I heard my name being called by that all too familiar voice.

"Fuck," I cursed under my breath. I tried to ignore him and continue to strap Brandon into his car seat. If this little boy wasn't so slow I could have avoided seeing Corey. I became even more irritated when I felt him standing behind me. I finished strapping my son in, making sure he was safe and secure. When I turned around Corey was invading my bubble. I took a step back bumping into the car.

"Hey Corey!" Brandon yelled. I watched Corey draft up a smirk on his face. I had one arm resting on the door while the other sat on the curve of my hip.

"Hey, wassup lil man." I rolled my eyes. I was ready to leave and he was holding me up.

"What you want Corey?" I asked him. Annoyance was defiantly heard in my voice.

"Where ya'll goin?" he asked looking inside my car at a couple duffle bags. I could kick myself for living out of the trunk of my car. I didn't want nor need him to know I was away from home.

"Back to D.C." I simply stated. He took a step back with his mouth agape.

"For good?" he asked.

"No, just for awhile; death in my family,"

"Oh damn, sorry to hear that."

"Uh huh. So what? What do you really want?"

"I've been tryna get up with you. Talk to you, I miss you." Did I miss him? Of course I did but I was not about to let him know. I couldn't even put my fingers on what exactly I missed about him. So I rolled my eyes at his confession.

"No you don't Corey," I told him.

"How the fuck you gonna tell me how I feel? I miss your ass. Why is it so hard for you to believe?"

"Because you not once showed me this fuckin—" I looked down at Brandon starring at us. I moved out of the doorway pushing Corey back a little and shutting the door so Brandon couldn't hear. "You haven't shown me attention since we been together. Now all of a sudden you wanna keep popping up at my house, calling me, texting me saying how much you miss me. Corey get that bullshit outa here!" I felt my face balled into this ugly scowl. Corey had this look of surprise on his face. He not once in the three years we were together heard me talk to him like that.

"I fuckin deserve better than how you were treating me. I don't need this stress. I don't need my son seeing his mama treated like shit. Nah, it ain't gonna happen." I told him. He knodded his head.

"Well lets start ova," he said. I shook my head as I tucked my lips inside of my mouth. He just didn't get it. It's hard to start over when I've already invested so many years into him. I wasn't interested in starting this madness over.

"I'm dead ass, when you coming back?"

"I don't know," I said as I sighed. He sucked his teeth.

"Well call me when ya'll come back" he said. "ya'll be safe."

"Aight Corey," I said while I got into the car. Just as I was about to shut the door I heard him yell. "And don't go fuckin nobody while you down there!"

Yasmine

"Boo can you finish getting Isaac ready," I yelled from the bathroom. I was trying to put my face on so that we could hurry up and go, but I still hadn't put Isaac's clothes on. I liked to wait until the last possible minute to put his clothes on because he always finds a way to dirty them up in the shortest amount of time.

We were making it a family day down at the Smithsonian. Fall was beginning to make itself known as the leaves turned all colors but green before carelessly falling to the ground; a slight breeze, sending everyone to fish for their jackets. I had to make sure Xavier was bundled down because I couldn't afford for him to get sick. He was the easiest to get sick, and I seriously was not lying. The wind could blow and he'd become congested, runny nose, a little fever.

I walked out of the bathroom rubbing lotion on my hands and headed into the front of the apartment where I knew the boys were.

"Ya'll ready?" I went into the coat closet and pulled out the boy's jacket. Xavier was sitting on the couch playing with this DS while Isaac lie on the floor with his foot stretched up to Robert, whom was tying his shoe.

"Yeah," Xavier said without looking up.

"Zay, you're not taking that game with you, so get up and go put it in your room and come put your jacket on." I watched him get up not paying attention trying to walk to his room, almost hitting the corner of the wall. He stopped for a minute, head still in the game.

"Xavier!" I raised my voice to him.

"Okay," he hurriedly put his game down and ran in his room. I looked up at the clock. We had ten minutes to get to the bus stop before the bus came.

"Come on ya'll before we miss the bus." I said.

"Why we don't just drive?"

"Do you have gas money or money to park?" Robert sucked his teeth. He was quick suggesting something but never have the money to go and do it. I rolled my eyes.

We made it outside just in time to see the bus about to turn the corner. It was early. About three minutes early. I couldn't stand public transportation. For one, they jacked the fairs up so much next thing we know, fairs were gonna be three dollars to ride, and it doesn't make it any better that they stopped giving out transfers. Metro sure do know how to make a killing, but no good workers.

We explored down town that day. Out of my whole twenty-six years of living in the district, I had never been to the monument, Capital or the Lincoln Memorial. I wanted my boys to experience DC young.

"Isaac and Xavier, stop all that damn running in this museum before ya'll knock something over. I ain't got money to be paying for nothing." I yelled after them. They slowed down and finally came to a halt in front of the reptile exhibit. Robert and I walked over, hand and hand, standing behind the boys as they began to have a million questions; especially Isaac.

"Xavier, what's that?" Isaac asked. Xavier stared at the display for a minute before stuttering the word out.

"P—py—umm," he paused studying the word. "Python," he said looking at us for reassurance.

"Yeah, it's a python," Robert said.

"They had a movie about this snake." I said as I pointed to the Anaconda.

"And what's that?" Isaac asked again.

"That's an Anaconda," I stated. The boys continued to gawk over the snakes as Robert phone began to go off. I kept my head straight but glanced over as he took his phone out of his pocket quickly trying to press ignore but not before I seen that it was his side bitch that was calling him. It was bad enough that she was calling him, but this nigga had the audacity to start texting her.

Malikaa

I was feeling like a brand new woman after I let Darious into my cookie jar. Holding off that long was well worth it. That night just made me realize how much built up sexual frustration I had in me. If he hadn't had to be to work in the morning I would have kept him trapped inside of my apartment trying every sex position known to man. I had brought a karma sutra book studying it like I was going to be quizzed on it.

I was dressed in sweat pants, a wife beater and my house slippers. It was my clean up day and I had every intention on spending my entire day on just cleaning. I had been neglecting my home for a few weeks and I could no longer deal with the filth. I was in my zone; I had Frank Ocean blaring through my speakers. I was so far into my music that I didn't hear someone banging on my door.

"Who the hell is bangin on my door like that?" I asked myself. I hated for people to bang on my door like the damn police. I was a fairly private when it came to my house and all that banging was inviting people to peak out of their door and be nosy. I swung my door open just in time to see my big headed younger brother about to bang on the door again. Lamar was a lot taller than me, and looked exactly like our mom. Long eyelashes, smooth caramel skin, he held my mom's height at five eight, but he had his daddies built; one hundred pounds soak and wet.

"What the fuck is your problem Lamar?" he put this dumb smirk on his face. I hated when he wore that smirk.

"I told him not to bang on your door like that." Robyn said as she moved into the house. I moved to the side so they can get into the house easily.

"Lamar, what the fuck you got on?" I asked as I shut the door and walked behind them. I walked over to by black leather couch and flopped down on it, tucking my legs under my butt. The couch was already worn, it was time for me to get a new one, I think I wanted to go with a gray suede couch next. I was almost done cleaning; I still had my room to tackle.

"Nigga, you too damn old to be tryna dress like these young boys." He had on these too small skinny jeans that only reached his hips and barely made his butt; exposing his plaid boxers. He looked like he pulled his whole outfit out of Robyn's closet because his shirt was just as tight as his jeans.

"I hope he catch a yeast infection on his balls." Robyn spat angrily. "Those my new jeans, I hadn't even worn those yet!"

"Why would you do that?" I asked him.

"I told her I'ma get her another pair," he said all the while going through my refrigerator. "She keeps bitchin bout these damn jeans I ain't gonna buy shit." I looked at him like he lost his damn mind, in fact, I know he lost it. He don't come out the side of his neck addressing his sister like that.

"Who the fuck you talkin to?" He didn't answer. "Don't get your head knocked off your shoulders. You don't talk to your sisters like we some bitches on the street you fuck." I looked at Robyn and her four month belly. She looked so miserable. Three months ago her intentions were to be pregnant free; but after her child's father persuaded her to keep the baby she had to come clean with my mom. I've never heard so many hoe's thrown around. My mom forgot that she was Robyn's age once. She was actually a year younger when she had me. Now Robyn is sitting in my living room, stress etched across her face because she hadn't seen or heard from her child's father in a month.

Joi

I walked into Darrell's office building ready to finally get my lunch date with him. I was not taking *'no, I have to work during my lunch,'* for an answer yet again. I brought lunch with me in case he cries about how much he really have to stay during lunch; we could have it in his office at the little coffee table on the left side of the room. I made sure I dressed in my one of his favorite business dresses that day. I put on my black pencil dress, red ski high stilettos with my red clutch and Armani shades. My hair, my hair was in a nice style like how Halle Barry's was in the movie *'Sword Fish'*.

The day I came home with my hair chopped off, Darrell was visibly upset, but didn't say anything. Every time he looked at me he just shook his head. He loved when my hair was long; once upon a time when we were intimate he loved to pull on it. Now we don't even get down with the get down so what was the reason for me to continuously have all that hair? I needed a change. I walked onto the elevator getting ready to go up to the third floor to where Darrell's office was located. Just as the elevator doors were about to close they stopped halfway as hands waved in between them opening the doors back up. I was intrigued by his mesmerizing orbs that I didn't realized he was talking to me.

"How you doin?" his voice was thick and filled with masculinity. I hadn't felt like I was feeling since the first year of Darrell's and I's first year of marriage. Like a little school girl being around her first crush. The air was on, but it was hot in that elevator.

"Hey," was all I could manage to get out.

"Mrs. Washington? Right?" I raised my eyebrow.

"Yes?" I said unaware of how he knew me.

"Sorry my name is Jamaal. I work for the same firm as your husband. I saw your beautiful picture on his desk awhile ago. I could never forget a beautiful face." I felt myself blushing.

"Well thank you," I didn't know what else to say. I hadn't intentionally flirted with someone since before I married so I was feeling quite awkward.

"So, you brought Mr. Washington some lunch huh?" I nodded my head.

"Yes, in case I can't pry him away from his desk. He's been so engulfed in this big case he's been working on it's hard to get him away from this office."

"Hmm," Jamaal said before looking forward.

Hmm? What the hell does hmm mean? I thought to myself. The elevator doors opened and he walked off. I looked at the top of the doors to see that we were at the third floor. I quickly exit the elevator before the doors had a chance to close on me.

"Jamaal," I called after him. He wasn't too far ahead of me so my call out to him was not too loud. Jamaal turned around to me sending me into an abrupt stop.

"Yes Mrs. Washington?"

"Joi," he smiled at me.

"Yes Joi?"

"What did *'hmm'* mean?" I wanted to know, I needed to know. Jamaal looked at me then he shifted his gaze over to the right.

"I just never heard about this big case, I work with him on majority of his cases and I'm sure I would know about this *big* case that appeared out of nowhere." I took in a deep breath and rolled my eyes before exhaling. I couldn't believe this shit. I knew Darrell's black ass was lying. I don't understand why men think women are dumb to their dirt. I know him; I know when he's lying. "But hey," Jamaal took his hand, cuffed my chin and made me look up at him. I knew I should be mad, I knew that I should have been trying to find a ways to catch Darrell in his lies; but the touch of Jamaal's hands, the warmth of his breath made my panties so damn wet. I shivered at his touch. I could just imagine how he would be flipping me around in his bedroom.

"I'm not one to break up a home. Maybe he is working on a big case, I donno. Don't let my comment ruin what ya'll have going on." I sighed. I rubbed my lips together, massaging my Mac into my lips.

"What are you doin for lunch?" I shocked myself by letting those words seep through my lips. He put a smirk on his gorgeous face.

"Well, Joi, I actually just came back from lunch but we can defiantly set something up, that is if your husband doesn't mind." He told me.

"Le me worry about my husband," I told him. I pulled the pen out of his suit pocket and wrote my number on his hand.

"Use it," I told him before walking off.

"Hi Mrs. Washington, you're here for Darrell?" Meagan, Darrell's preppy receptionist asked. Meagan was two years fresh out of high school when she got the job at the receptionist. She was a cheerleader in high school so I assume that's where all the prep in her voice came from. It was quite annoying to me.

"Yes Meagan honey. He in his office?" I asked. I stood in front of her desk and spoke with her. She was in all actuality a sweet girl, very bright. She wanted to go to college but couldn't afford the tuition, then she just became comfortable with the pay and college was an afterthought.

"Yes, he's in there with Ms. Austin," she told me.

"Ms. Austin?" I asked a bit confused.

"Yes, Stephanie Austin," I nodded her head.

"Alright, I'll talk to you later Meagan," I waved by and made my way back to Darrell's office. I didn't bother to knock on the door before opening it. I looked at the both of them, Darrell and Stephanie, as they both looked up at me from their paper work.

"Joi, what are you doing here?" Darrell asked me.

"I came to bring you to lunch with me." Stephanie shifted her eyes from me over to the big window behind them. He looked over at Stephanie before asked her to leave the office. Once she was gone and his door was closed, he spoke.

"I can't, I promised Stephanie that we'd go to lunch and discuss this case." I ran my tongue over my teeth.

"Damn Darrell, you act like you fuckin the bitch," I said as I looked at him with arched eyebrows. "Are you?"

"No Joi damn," he based at me. I gave a small chuckle to myself as I folded my arms over my breast.

"Yeah, okay D. I'm so tired of you lyin to me,"

"I'm not leaving the office for lunch Joi, so I guess I'll see you when I get home." I nodded my head. I wasn't in the mood to continuously argue with him, I was throwing in the towel and ridding myself of the mess he's created of our marriage.

Jalissa

I pulled up to the house that I was all too familiar with. The colonial style home was neatly groomed. The outside of the house had no leaves on the ground, no debris anywhere near the front of the house. Scooters and bicycles lay in the middle of the lawn. I looked at myself in the rearview mirror making sure every strand of my hair was in place. I looked back at Brandon to see that he was still sleeping. I did not want to wake him up out of his nap. He was going to be so grumpy for at least an hour, maybe two. I sighed before getting out the car and wrapping my peacoat around my body. I knew they were going to be so shocked to see me here; if not my size alone. When I first left I was well over two hundred and fifty pounds. After giving birth to Brandon, I was determined to lose my baby weight as well as all that extra baggage. I had lost almost one hundred pounds, so I know they were going to be looking at me astonished.

I went in the back and pulled Brandon in my arms. I had to stop for a minute as we made our way to the door as the wind almost knocked us over. I had to make sure his face was covered. Although this wind was nothing compared to

Chicago, I still wanted to make sure he had no opportunity to catch a cold. I knocked on the door as I made sure Brandon's face was tucked away in my neck.

"Grandma, the door!" I heard a child scream. It was a little girls' voice, thick and heavy. I knew that voice from anywhere. She was the one I had grown so attached to.

"Get away from the door. Madison, get your sister and ya'll come and get this stuff up from out the middle of the floor." I heard my mother yell. Her voice made me cringe but I missed hearing it. A few seconds later I was face to face with an older mirrored image of myself. She had a few more gray hairs than I remembered, other than that she still looked the same. My mom stood five-nine, and slim; but had a gut that was inherited from four children and ample amount of beer. She kept her hair short, if not a fade like most men wear their hair, then it was kept at the length Fantasia kept her hair when she first came out.

"Look who we have here," my mom said with a wide smile painted on her face. I smiled at her. She moved out of the way so that I could come into the house. I shifted Brandon in my arms as I looked around the house. Everything was still the same, just a few pictures new pictures. "Who's that

Benny?" I heard someone ask my mom.

"Who it look like?" my mom asked back.

"Girl," the woman with the salt and pepper dreads slapped her leg and twisted in her seat. "That's your daughter. For real?" My mom nodded her head. "Girl, come here," the lady was talking to me. I walked over to her. "Girl, I bet you don't remember me. Last time I seen you were as small as that baby in your arms." I smiled at her. She was right. I had no idea who she was. "How old are you now?"

"Twenty-five" I stated.

"Umm, grown woman now," I nodded my head

"How old is the baby?"

"Three,"

"Boy or girl?" she was asking a lot of questions and I was just ready to sit down and relax for awhile.

"Boy," I said as I began to take Brandon stuff off. I looked down and wiped his forehead. He was sweating.

"Look at my grandbaby," my mom said as she came over and took him out of my arms. I was relieved because he was heavy. He squirmed in her arms. I smiled at the sight of them two. It was refreshing to be in my childhood home. I sat and talked to them until I felt myself being shaken out of my sleep. I hadn't known I fell asleep. I must have been extremely tired. I had awakened to little hands touching my face. I had one pair poking at my cheeks and the other trying to open my eyelids. I snatched my head back away from them and looked at them like they were crazy. I looked at Madison and Brandon. I already could feel the trouble that was bound to brew from the two of them being together.

I picked up my phone to check the time only to see that I received two missed calls and a text message from Corey.

From: Corey
Sent: Friday, October 20, 2012
7:45pm
Hey, yall make it?

I ignored it. I wanted to take this time to sort things out with him. Clear my head and figure out what it was that I really wanted to do. I was so sure that I wanted to leave him alone and start fresh, but after seeing him that morning; I just didn't know anymore.

"You eat?" I asked Brandon. He nodded his head yes. I looked at him before looking around the now empty living room. I heard my mom and some other people in the kitchen talking. I knew that Brandon was okay so I rolled back on my side and drifted back off to sleep.

*

The next day I had a busy day planned. I woke up early got myself and Brandon dressed and headed out. Our first stop was Ihop. He was hungry and I hated fast food breakfast. I would usually stop at a little diner because I know they serve real food there but I didn't know of any in the area. We sat out in the waiting area waiting for our name to be called. I never knew all the blood could drain from my face as fast as it did. I tried to look at everything except for the woman coming my way. I was hoping that she would just walk past me and out of the door. But with the luck that I was having she came and stood right in front of me. Her wide hips blocked my view of everything else around me. He looked just like her, and Brandon looked just like him. He was indeed an Anderson.

"Jalissa, hey honey! I haven't seen you in so long," I smiled at her.

"I know, how are you?" I asked. I was trying to be polite. As far as I knew, she had no knowledge of the broken bones, black eyes and heart ache her son had given me.

"I'm well, how have you been?" Ms. Holt looked at me with her mysterious orbs. You can never know what she was thinking. Terrence had those exact eyes. That's why I never knew when he was going to strike me.

"I'm— " Brandon cut me off.

"Mommy, I'm huuuunnnnnnggg rrrrrry," Brandon whined. I sighed. I swear children always knew the right moment to say something.

"Aight ma, you ready?" I closed my eyes. I knew her voice from anywhere. I couldn't stand her. Her being Terrence older sister Alice, short for Allyson. She was three years older than me, two years older than Terrence. I don't know what it was, but she never, and I mean *never* liked me. Even before he and I had gotten together.

"Alight, Alice you remember Jalissa don't you?" she asked.

"Uh huh," was all she said. I rolled my eyes at her and took my attention back down to a squirming Brandon. He was so antsy. We had been sitting there for fifteen minutes and knowing him, he was ready to get up and run around.

"Mommy?" Ms. Holt asked.

"Yes, this is Brandon. He's three." I stated nervously yet with pride.

"Hmm," Alice said.

"Hmm what?" I asked Alice.

"Girls, now is neither the time nor place to be arguing." Ms. Holt said trying to mediate.

"Does Terrance know?" Alice asked me. She was always trying to start something. Why couldn't they just leave me alone and go on about their business.

"Know what? I haven't talked or seen him in all of three years. And I wish not to talk or see him." I told her.

"It's best you tell him before I do," she said.

"You not gonna do nothing Allyson," Ms. Holt said. "That's between Terrance and Jalissa. I just know one thing," Ms. Holt looked at me. "I better be seeing my grandson more than every three years. And have him to give me a call every day." She said.

"How you know that this is Terrance son?" I asked her. She gave me this dumbfounded look.

"He looks just like Terrance when he was his age. Besides, I know. I knew when you first got pregnant. You probably didn't, but I knew. I just thought you got rid of the pregnancy."

"I didn't know I was pregnant until I was long gone and damn near about to have him." I told her truthfully. "I'll tell him," I sighed. "Just let me, give me a little time. I'll let him know before I leave to go back home." I told her. Before her or Alice had a chance to say anything else my name was being called. She didn't let me leave before giving me her phone number and making me promise that I would bring Brandon by to spend some time with her.

Yasmine

"Ugh!" I yelled as I called Robert's phone for the umpteenth time and each time it went straight to voicemail. He was doing either two things. He was hitting ignore or his bitch was hitting ignore. I knew it wasn't off because it rung twice before going to voicemail. I flopped down on the sofa and sighed. I was so through with his lying ass. I had never been so fed up with someone before in my life, but him. He always had to be first in my book for something. I always tried to figure out why I bothered with him. I looked at the clock on the cable box and seen it was going on one in the afternoon.

I scrolled through my phone to see who I could call. Eight years later, I still didn't understand how this motherhood thing worked out. Childless weekend and I still never had anything to do. "I should see what Malikaa is doin," I said to myself. Just as I was about to push *'talk'* on my phone someone knocked on my door. I walked over to the door and opened it without asking who was on the other end. So irresponsible of me.

"What the hell!" I said in pure shock. Standing in front of me was the only female that was not of any blood to me that I would consider my sister.

"Surprise!" she said. I grabbed her into a hug. I looked down to her left, my right.

"Is this my g-baby?" I asked excitedly.

"Uh huh, say hi Brandon," he waved at me. I picked him up, he just stared at me.

"Hey cutie," I said. "Um, he looks just like his daddy."

"Girl, it's chilly in this hall. Can I come in?"

"Oh my bad," I said as I moved out of the doorway. Jalissa went and sat on the loveseat. I went and sat on the sofa. She had Brandon bundled up like there was a blizzard outside.

"Really Lisa? It's not damn cold outside." She laughed. "He sweatin,"

"Girl, I don't have time for him and those colds. His lil dry boogers be terrible." She laughed.

"What you doin back? I thought you said you were never stepping foot back in the DMV."

"Rob ain't tell you?" she asked me. I was clueless.

"What happened?" I asked.

"My grandfather died yesterday morning." She told me. My heart dropped. I wondered if Robert knew yet.

"Damn, I'm sorry to hear that." I didn't know what else to say. What do you really tell a person when someone close to them has passed?

"Yeah," was all she said. "Where is Rob anyway?"I rolled my eyes.

"Girl, I'm so done with his black ass."

"No you not," she said.

"I'm serious,"

"No, ya'll gettin married. I have the maid of honor speech wrote out and everything!"

"You had that speech since we was seventeen, it's old and ashy. You can write another one." She laughed. I sat Brandon down and he ran to Isaac's toys that he had in the corner.

"What he do this time?"

"Same shit. I mean stuff. You know Erica?" I asked her.

"Naw, who is she?"

"You know her if you see her. She lives by your mom. Anyway, he fuckin her. Now the broad got my numba and keep playin on my phone." I told her. I felt my blood boiling.

"How she get your numba?"

"Rob's dumb self called me from her phone," she looked at me with a straight face. The same face I gave Robert when he told me the same thing. "I seriously can't take him anymore, it's seriously time for me to move on. That young girl can have him. He thinks I'm stupid, keep ignoring my calls today."

"Umm, well when you leave him, leave him for good." She told me.

"We better off as friends." I told her. She nodded her head. I had to update her on what was going on with everyone.

"Oh, girl let me tell you what's going on since you been gone. You know Malikaa talkin to this nigga name Rashaad that down in VA doin three years,"

"Umm, what he doin three years for?"

"Robery I think." I said. "Anyway, well you know she messin with Darious,"

"Darious who?"

"Your cousin Darious,"

"Wassup with ya'll and my family members?" she asked. I shrugged my shoulders.

"She fuckin Darious and him or Rashaad don't know about nothin about each other."

"She gonna get what's comin to her ass. Watch."

"That ain't it. I know you can't stand Joi or her husband; but girl! So Malikaa call me and tell me that Darrell is cheatin on Joi." Lisa's eyes nearly fell out the sockets.

"You lyin?" she asked.

"Darrell invited the chick that Joi thinks he's cheatin on her with to the house for dinner. Then a few weeks later Joi pops up at the job and catch the chick in his office. They weren't doing anything but it's the fact that she was in his office with the door closed. But, but wait there is more,"

"More?"

"Yes! Joi is messin with one of the men from the firm."

"Girl, what the hell is goin on with ya'll."

"No, that's them," I told her. Her friendship with Joi was still a touchy subject for her so I jumped to another topic. We sat, watched Brandon play around until he got hungry and then figured out what we were gonna eat. We debated what we wanted until we settled on Ruby Tuesday. I wanted a Ruby Relaxer and Lisa wanted one of those Texas teas. So to Ruby Tuesday we went.

*

I sat across from Lisa and Brandon. I had no intentions on letting her know that Joi and Malikaa were on their way to the restaurant. I had every intention on this reunion being good, but something in me was telling me that all hell was about to break loose. I looked over at the entrance of the restaurant then glanced over at Lisa whose head was stuck in the menu. Brandon was busy coloring the coloring sheet that they provided.

"Umm, that's what I needed to tell you earlier. Guess who I ran into," Lisa said as she slapped her menu on the table. I raised my eyebrow. "Terrance mom and sister,"

"What happened?" I asked. Alice and Lisa couldn't stand each other for reasons unknown to everyone.

"His sister was about to make me bash her skull in. I don't like that hoe."

"Why ya'll can't stand each other?"

"I'll tell you later, just know it got something to do with my brother." I knodded my head. "Yeah, so his mom was like she knows Brandon is her grandson. He looks just like Terrance when he was that age. Alice gonna tell me that I better tell him before she does." My jaw dropped.

"You gonna tell him." She shrugged her shoulders.

"I don't know. I don't have time to go down that road with him again. If I tell him it's gonna be in a public place." I knew all about their situation. I tried as hard as I could to get her away from him, but it had gotten to the point that I had to clean my hands of their drama. She had to leave him when she was good and ready. I couldn't make that decision for her. I'm glad she left him before he killed her though.

"Well if it ain't Miss. Jalissa." I heard Malikaa say. I looked up and seen her and Joi standing above our table. Jalissa put on a smile and got up to hug Malikaa. I scooted over so they could get in the booth with me.

"Hey Malikaa and Joi," I said. They both said hi. I heard Malikaa whisper something to Joi.

"No, I see she sittin ova there. I'm not bout to sit here and act fake and phony cause she sittin in front of me."

"Aw shit," I mumbled. Jalissa cut her eyes at her.

"I don't have to speak Malikaa. I don't like her, and whateva friendship there was is nonexistent now."

"Joi, I don't know what you have up your ass but I ain't ask you to speak to me. You see I ain't say shit to you cause as you can see you're not a factor in my life. If you want to continue to sit and bitch, cry and moan cause you don't want to speak to me go right ahead but just know I don't give a fuck. I'm too grown to sit here and argue with you and all of your pettiness. You go ahead and continue to be bitter." Lisa said. I just looked straight ahead. The rest of the dinner was quiet with the occasional talking that I engaged in from time to time with Malikaa. The tension was so thick.

*

I got home around ten that night. I stayed up and watched TV until about two that morning and

Robert's ass still wasn't home. I sighed as I turned over about to close my eyes when I heard keys in the door. I instantly rolled my eyes. I heard as he made his way in the bedroom; taking off his clothes making all the noise in the world and climbed in bed with me. He tried to wrap his arms around me but I pushed him off.

"Yo Yesi what the fuck?" He asked as his voice boomed off of the walls.

"Go back to that hoe you was fucking and cuddle up with that bitch." I said as I closed my eyes.

"What the fuck, I'm not fuckin no body but you." He stated to me as if I cared.

"Yeah okay Robert. Oh and tell yo bitch to stop callin my phone before I knock her teeth down her throat." I heard him suck his teeth before turning his back to me.

It had been years since I felt butterflies flutter. Just by his smile alone I felt like I was interacting with my first crush. I knew it was wrong stepping out on my marriage, but he was doing the exact same. Did I have proof? Well, no; but it was bound to come out. What's done in the dark shell soon come to light.

I guess I better listen to my last statement.

Jamaal and I sat across from each other enjoying a night out at Blues Alley down in Georgetown. It was refreshing to be out on a date. He held my hand in his as the saxophone made love to everyone's ears. I looked over and smiled at him. Jamaal was an all around perfect guy, I couldn't find anything wrong. He was stood in the same financial status that I was use to, car, home, no strings or baggage attached to him. I was always laughing and happy when I was with him. I was sure he was my tall dark and handsome knight in shining armor ready to come and save me. He knew my situation, knew I had a child and was married; but he didn't care. And I wondered if I should be worried about that. Jamaal wined and dined me for three months never pressuring me or hinting to me that he wanted some booty. I studied his face as he vibe with the music. I wanted to know what his ultimate goal was. Aside from just having a husband, I also had a daughter that I had to protect. I waited until the music number was over and the band was taking a break.

"You okay?" Jamaal asked. "You don't seem yourself tonight."

"What's your intentions?" I asked him.

"Huh?" he was confused.

"Why are you being so nice? Taking me out, the dinners, movies; things that couples do, minus having sex."

"What was your point in giving me your number if you didn't want me to try and pursue something with you?"

"But you know my situation,"

"Yeah, I know you're married; and so do you. What's the point?"

"I'm just stuck," he nodded his head. "I've been spending so much time with you in these past months; I don't want to catch these feelings. I'm still married. I have a family."

"So what you really tryna get at?" he asked me. I really didn't know. I shrugged my shoulders and took a deep breath. I rubbed my lips together before speaking.

"Ugh, this was just supposed to be about me getting back at Darrell for neglecting me. I was not suppose to get these damn feelings for you." I diverted my gaze away from him and looked over at the table next to us.

"But you did, what you gonna do bout it?" I was literally stuck between a rock and a hard place. I never imagined that I'd be in a place where I questioned the trust and faith in my mirage.

"I don't know," I told him. He took a deep breath, "I don't know Jamaal. I just need some time to figure out what road I want to take. If I was in this alone I'd be like 'hell yeah, let me take my chances.' But I'm not. I have Camille to think about." He nodded his head. He leaned forward then took my hand in his.

"I'll tell you what, let's just enjoy the night. We'll discuss our plans with each other at another time." I smiled at him as he kissed my hand. I had a big decision to make and I know I needed to make it sooner than later.

*

"Camille come sit down. Runnin round this house like you done lost your damn mind." Camille quickly came to a halt as she was running back from the bedroom. She was playing around with Malikaa's white Yorkie, in which she decided to name Snow White.

"Girl, leave her alone. She okay." Malikaa said to me.

"No she need to learn. Her damn daddy always letting her run around like a banshee." I was irritated. My home life and relationship matters were frustrating me and I found myself taking it out on everyone.

"You need penis," she told me laughing.

"Shut up, just cause you dippin and dabbin in places you ain't got no business dippin and dabbin,"

"Don't hate. You can be letting your frustrations out too if you forget bout that prune and hop on that dark chocolate that's been takin you out." I rolled my eyes at her.

"You think I don't want to hop on Jamaal every time I see him. Girl, I never knew my panties could get that soaked by just starin at a nigga." I let out. She made a sour face.

"You must not be lookin at the right nigga."

I rolled my eyes. "But see, I take commitment serious. I take my marriage serious. I'm not bout to go fuck Jamaal just cause I'm still sitting on my accusations."

"You trippin, I'd fuck the hell outa Jamaal. Have you literally seen him?"

"MeMe, Darious laid it down a few times and you don't know how to act," she laughed.

"A few times? Girl, every night of the month except for one week out of the month. I'ma have to sit in a tub full of vinegar the week before Rashaad come home." We burst into laughter.

"What's goin on with you and Rashaad anyway?"

"Don't act like you interested. I know you don't give to eff words about him," she was right, I didn't.

"I don't, but I still wanna know. He is your boo thang."

"Well if you must know, I haven't spoken to

him in a few weeks, almost a month." She confessed. I raised my eyebrow to her. "They probably on lock down,"

"Just hearin the work lock down make me think of that movie. It was so said when lil dude got killed. They rapped the poor child." After seeing that movie, I believed that any man that was in jail for longer than a year was someone's bitch or had a bitch. I didn't want to mention that to her though because her man had passed that year mark a little while ago.

"Uh huh," was all she said.

"Anyway, have you talked to Yesi?" I wanted to change the subject.

"Yeah, she was chillin with Lisa," I rolled my eyes at just the mention of her name. Lisa and I were as close as close could get. We were best friends since sophomore year, but life happened, we grew up and men came into our lives.

"You know her granddad died,"

"Damn," was all I knew to say. I wanted to call her and see how she was doing because I knew what it was like to have someone close pass away, but I was stubborn and didn't want to have anything to do with her. "Well let me get goin. I gotta get Camille home so she can do this homework."

"Alight honey," Malikaa said as she stood up with me. I called Camille into the living room and Snow White came trotting behind her. They were so cute together. I thought about getting her a puppy because another child was nowhere in the future.

"Alight MeMe I'm gone." I said as I swung the door open. I stopped in my tracks as I seen this tall peanut butter toned slender man standing in the doorway getting ready to knock on the door. His dreads hung past his shoulders, pulled back by two strands of his own hair.

It was Rashaad.

I looked back at Malikaa and seen the priceless expression on her face. If only I could know what's going through her head right now. I leaned over and whispered to her,

"You want me to go get that vinegar now?"

Malikaa

"What, when did you get out?" I asked him pulling out of his embrace. To say I was surprised would be an understatement. "You wasn't to get out until the beginning of the year."

"I wanted to surprise you," his voice was sex; so deep and masculine. Just hearing him speak got me wanting to jump all over him.

"I am surprised. When did you get out?" I asked again.

"Last Monday," I gave him wide eyes and slapped him on his arm. Snow White growled and started barking. Rashaad looked down at her. "You got yourself a lil ankle biter," I picked her up and put her in her little cage and then came back and sat beside him.

"Why you just now comin to see me?" he gave me his breathtaking smile. His smile is what made me fall in love with him.

"Sorry, I had to spend some time with my muva. You know after today you bout to have me locked up in that room. Or better yet, I'm bout to have you locked in that room." I laughed. He locked eyes with me and I began to blush. Darious was the furthest thing from my mind as I sat with Rashaad.

"Are you hungry baby?"I asked him.

"Nah, I just left from my moms house and she had cooked. She been cookin my favorites all week." I smiled. I couldn't control my urges.

His lips, those plump juicy pink lips of his.

I pulled his face to mine and tongue wrestled him. I didn't want to let him up for air. We began to go at it like two horny teenagers. Clothes thrown all over my living room, slurping and slapping sounds filled the apartment. I was an acrobat that night. I never knew my limbs could bend so far back; and Rashaad with all that stamina. I tried pulling away because, well, I was tired. But no, he pulled my little ass back and continued to give it to me; and I took it. Night came and our body laid tangled restlessly in my white sheets. My phone vibrated. I looked to my left to see that it was not on my night stand so I let it ring. Whoever was calling would get the picture when they realized that I wasn't picking up the phone. I could hear the faint snores of Rashaad. I watched him until my eyes were just as heavy as the hold that he had on my waist.

We slept until the sun rose, brightening my pale walls. I hopped out of bed as my eyes adjusted to the light. It took a minute for me to realize that it was Monday morning. We literally had sex the entire weekend, only stopping to pay the Chinese man for our food. I knew that I would need the entire week to recuperate. I didn't think my love muffin could endure another stroke.

8:35am

I was late for work.

I technically wasn't late yet, but by time I made it uptown I would be late as hell. I snatched my phone off of the dresser as I tripped into my closet.

"Shit! I need to clean this damn room. I'm bout to break my damn neck." I said. I quickly called my supervisor. I knew the Michelle would be pissed that I was running late. She was always whining about making it to work on time because time is money, but hell, shit happens. I was relieved when she didn't answer the phone because I didn't want to speak directly to her. I left a quick message letting her know I was running late but I was in route.

I couldn't move as fast as I wanted so I moved

as fast as my thighs would allow. By time I got to work I was every bit of two hours late. I knew a write up was coming. Any other time I would stand around and chit chat with all the other people in the office as we made our cups of coffee, but not that day. I couldn't afford any more attention drawn to me. The day crept by. I was use to getting text messages all day from Darious. He had called me over ten times, and not once did I answer. I missed hearing his voice and his conversations. I had to text him.

To: Darious
Sent: Monday, October 20, 2012
12:50pm
Hey Darious

To: Lika
Sent: Monday, October 20, 2012
12:55pm
Ur alive

To: Darious
Sent: Monday, October 20, 2012
12:55pm
Um yea! I miss u!

To: Lika

Sent: Monday, October 20, 2012

1:0\2pm

Do u? I called u all wkend. U was duckin me

To: Darious

Sent: Monday, October 20, 2012

1:05pm

Nooooo, I jus wanted some me time. Can I have that?

To: Lika

Sent: Monday, October 20, 2012

1:10pm

uh huh...u can have w/e u want

To: Darious

Sent: Monday, October 20, 2012

1:10pm

o really...well I wanna see u

To: Lika

Sent: Monday, October 20, 2012

1:12pm

I'll see what I could do. I might come by 2night

I smiled but then thought about how Rashaad was still at my place.

To: Darious

Sent: Monday, October 20, 2012

1:15pm

umm, how bout we go to ur house tonight

To: Lika

Sent: Monday, October 20, 2012

1:15pm

Im not makin double trips. U betta bring work clothes.

Jalissa

I drove up to this Catholic Church off of eastern avenue after the funeral. The repast was being held in the banquet hall, so I skipped going to the grave site and made my way there to make sure everything was set up properly. My mom had Brandon so that took a little stress off of me while I got everything in order for when the large crowd walked in. the reception wasn't as festive as the past receptions we had. Maybe it was because of who it was that we had laid to rest, or it could have been because of the person who organized the whole thing. The atmosphere was so strict you couldn't move without it being scheduled.

My grandma and Brandon was restless and I, well I was bored; so I hopped up when they asked for a volunteer to take my grandma home. My grandma was one of a kind. So head strong, stern, yet so sweet.

"You okay grandma?" I asked as we stopped as a red light. The church wasn't too far away from the house.

"Yeah, grandma just tired baby," she glanced

over her shoulder back at Brandon. I did the same to see that he was back there fighting his sleep. I turned to 102.3 and let the oldies mellow out the silence in the car. I had too much on my mind and didn't feel like talking about it or anything for that matter. Corey and I had been texting and calling each other since I had been away, I was seriously considering giving him another chance. I didn't want to get to know another person all over again. I rather make things work. Then there I was in DC, been there for almost a week and had yet to tell Terrence about Brandon. I already knew Alice had told him that's why I wasn't surprise, nor shocked when I seen his truck parked out front. After three years he still had that green Pilot.

"Who's that in front of the house?" Grandma asked. I sighed deeply. It felt like a thousand poisonous butterflies swarming at the pit of my stomach. The last time I seen him was not good. I had never seen my face so swollen and I still til this day never knew what I did that continuously triggered the monster in him. He wasn't always like that, but Joi warned me about him because she knew him longer. But I was too hard headed and, I had to experience things for myself.

"Umm, you remember Terrence? The guy I was with before I left?" she shook her head no. "Oh, well he's my ex and that's Brandon's fava."

"Oh, so what's wrong go take the baby to see the man." I put the car in park and rubbed my hands on my temples. I was beginning to stress.

"Grandma he don't know bout Brandon." Grandma gave me this look that said I was the dumbest person she has ever seen. "Mama, you don't know what I had to go through with him." She left the conversation alone. That's one thing I loved about that woman. She knew when to cut the conversation short and not carry on. She proceeded to get out of the car.

"I'll see you when you come inside. I'm bout to go take me two pm's and go lay down." She was about to shut the door but then poked her head back in and said, "Bring that baby in the house, its cold out here and he's sleepy."

"Okay," Reality set in that I was finally about to interact with Terrance after three long fearless years. I always imagined what it what be like, what I would say and do when I see him; but I knew that I would be doing none of that. I turned my car off and waited for a minute trying to gather my thoughts before getting out and going to the back seat taking Brandon out. There was no way that I could ignore him because he was sitting directly in front of the house. I had to walk past his car in order to walk up the drive way. I couldn't even step foot on the drive way good before he hopped his tall red ass out the car. He had gained weight since the last time I saw him, he had to of been at least two hundred ninety-five pounds to three hundred pounds. I'd be lying if I said he didn't look good. His jet black low cut fade. He always did like to keep his hair cut because if it had grown out he'd look like the male version of the orphan Annie.

After being with him for two in a half years but knowing him for all of five years, I knew the look on his face was nothing nice. My nerves were going crazy. I stood in front of him, but far enough so he couldn't touch me without reaching. I held Brandon in my arms. Terrance shook his head before speaking.

"Alice told me but I had to come see the shit for myself." I looked away from his glare. "A fuckin kid Lisa? And you aint tell me?" His voice held so much power. I jumped at the base that it held. I rubbed my lips together trying to calm my nerves.

"I was gonna tell you Terrance. I swear I was." I looked at him. His eyes read stress, confusion and anger.

"When?" I didn't say anything. "When he turn eighteen?" I actually didn't plan to tell him. I had no intentions on him finding out about Brandon. I was hoping that I'd find a man, fall in love and he welcomes me and my son in with open arms. We marry and he takes on the roll of daddy.

"No Terrance damn!" I shouted. I tried to make my voice sound confident. "I was gonna tell you, I just didn't know when."

"You lyin. You forgot that I know you, every inch of you."

"I didn't know I was pregnant until late in my pregnancy. And what did you honestly expect me to do when I found out I was pregnant Tee? You didn't want kids, and I wasn't coming back down here to you for you to keep beatin my ass."

"No I ain't want kids, but I wouldn't have made yo ass get a abortion! We woulda handle it." I shook my head. "Oh, so I take it some otha nigga raisin my son huh?"

"Why?" I shifted Brandon in my arms. He was heavy.

"What the fuck you mean why Jalissa? That's my fuckin son." He shouted. Brandon looked up at

Terrance. His face held a scowl.

"This is exactly why I didn't want you knowing about him. He is not bout to grow up with your habits Terrance."

"My habits, really Lisa?" I nodded my head. "You act like I put my fuckin hands on you every day,"

"I don't care how many times you did it; the fact is that you beat my ass. I had to walk around with fuckin black eyes and shit!"I heard a door open. I looked at the house and seen my grandma coming out the house. She came up to me and snatched Brandon away from me. She put him down so he could walk. She looked at the both of us.

"I told you to bring this baby in the house. It's too damn cold out here and then ya'll sittin out here arguing in front of him. That's just unhealthy. Ya'll stand out hea in this cold and let ery body else and this neighborhood know yo business if you want." My grandma turned on her heels and took Brandon along with her in the house. I rolled my eyes and folded my hands over my chest.

"Jalissa," I looked down at the ground and started kicking the imaginary rocks.

"What?"

"Jalissa, look at me." He took his cold hands and turned my head up to face him. "I apologize if I ever hurt you. For puttin my hands on you and anything else that I did that made you lose your trust in me." he said. I shook my head and moved his hand away from me.

"It's gonna take more than an apology for me to even come close to forgiving you. I don't think you realize what you put me through." I told him.

"Just let me raise my son, please." He was so sincere.

"I don't trust you Terrance,"

"I'm not askin for you to get back with me Lisa, I'm just askin to be in my sons life." I sighed. Not too many men begged to be in their child's life. I looked at him and rolled my eyes.

"I guess Tee." I said. He exhaled a breath that neither he nor I knew he was holding. He smirked at me.

"You look good. You lost weight and let your hair grow out. You know I always liked when your hair was long and curly."

"Thanks," I didn't know how to take his behavior.

"When do ya'll leave?"

"Thursday," he nodded his head.

"You happy?" he asked. I looked up at him.

"Yes I am. Are you happy?" He laughed.

"Why must you forget that I know you Lisa. Down to the way arch your back when I'm hittin it right." I shifted uncomfortably. "I know you not happy in your relationship Lisa,"

"Terrance, please, we're not goin there. Brandon is the subject matter here." He licked his two toned lips; half pink and half black, nodding his head.

"Aight, what's middle name?" he asked.

"Avante'," He scrunched up his face. "Brandon Avante' Anderson,"

"Umm, so I got someone to carry on the Anderson name," I chuckled. I dug my phone out of my coat pocket because it kept vibrating. I looked and seen that it was from Yasmine. I answered it.

"Lisa, get yo ass to my house cause I'm bout to

fuck yo cousin and his bitch up!" she screamed. My eyes grew big.

"What happened?"

"The bitch just went postal on my fuckin car."

"What the hell? Okay, I'm on my way." I told her then hung up the phone. I looked at Terrance as I fished my keys out of my pocket. "I gotta go. You remember my friend Yasmine right,"

"Yeah,"

"Well, something is goin on at her house with my cousin and this girl he messin with." I told him.

"Aight, well I'll take you ova there." I just looked at him. "No funny business Lisa. I just want to catch up with you and hopefully take you to dinner tonight,"

"And your son?"

"Nah, just us tonight, I want the whole day with him tomorrow before ya'll leave." He said. I was so skeptical on getting in the truck with him, but I did it anyway. I was praying that he didn't kill my ass, cut me into pieces and throw me in a ditch somewhere.

Yasmine

We laid under each other after we'd just got finish getting it in. I didn't want to move out of the spot where our bodies were marinating. I honestly couldn't move from that spot, that's just how good he put it on me. I looked at him as I laid my head on his chest. His eyes were fixed on the TV. Some college football game was on.

"What?" he asked without taking his eyes off of the TV.

"Nothing, just admiring you; thinkin bout how much I love you." I told him honestly.

"Yeah, I know." He rubbed his hand on his chin. I shook my head.

"You see us bein together long?" I was curious.

"Why not? We been together this long." he said. I watched his phone contionusly light up. It had been going off since we had gotten to the house from dripping the boys off at my brother house and it was killing my mood. I tried to ignore it because it was my time with him, but it was really getting under my skin.

"Yup, me you and Erica." He sucked his teeth.

"Comeon man," he started. "We havin a nice lil time and you always find a fuckin way to bring her up. I told you I wasn't fuckin that girl no more." I sat up letting the sheets fall from my chest. I threw on his shirt.

"You's a got damn lie Robert. I'm not fuckin stupid!" I yelled at him. "You sit and talk to the bitch while you wit me. Sendin the bitch shit like, 'Ima pound that pussy when I get there.'"

"Yo insecure ass, get out my face wit all that bullshit young." He was caught and he knew it.

"Bullshit?" my phone rang. I wasn't gonna answer it but I seen that it was his bitch on the side. "Speaking of the bitch, look who callin my fuckin phone," I turned the phone to him so that he could witness. His face was priceless, all the blood rushed from his face. I answered it.

"Why the fuck you callin my phone?"

"I didn't call for you. Tell Robert to come outside." She said.

"This not his fuckin phone, if you want him call his damn phone." I hung up on her. My blood was boiling. His hoe was taking it to the next level, calling my phone looking for him. Was I now the side joint?

"How the fuck she know where I live Robert?" I was beyond furious.

"I don't know. She probably just tryna play you." All of a sudden I heard a loud crash and a car alarm going off. I looked at Robert wide eyed and he hopped off the bed and ran to the window in the living room. Dick running freely and everything. My first reaction when I seen the big ass rock through my front windshield was to knock Robert up aside his head. I just began swinging on him. He tried to restrain me and block my hits but I was getting him good.

"I don't give a flyin fuck where you go, but get all your shit and get out my got damn house." I screamed. I heard another window break followed by,

"I know you in that bitch house. Bring yo black ass out!" My adrenaline was rushing. Neither one of them put an ounce of money into that car, that was all my hard work. I ran into the back room and threw on some sweat pants my tennis shoes and a bra under the shirt I was already wearing. As I made my way for the door Robert passed me trying to find something of his own to chase after me. I ran downstairs calling Lisa and Malikaa. Lisa didn't answer the first two times and Malikaa was in the middle of fucking when I called her. Which one, I don't know. When I finally got in touch with Lisa I threatened Rob's life, and I was at my breaking point so I was serious about carrying out my plans. He didn't know who he was dealing with because I was not the Yasmine that he supposedly fell in love with. I was the Yasmine that was fed up with his bullshit, stayed with him through *all* the things he put me through, through his downs and his lint filled pockets.

I threw my hair in a ponytail as I speed my way over to my car. "Bitch have you lost yo motha-fuckin mind?"

"Where the the hell is Robert?" she asked with her left hand on her hip and her right hand gripping the wooden baseball bat that she used to bust my side windows. I wanted to walk up to her and swing, but she had that bat and had a tight grip on it.

"This not Roberts got damn car. He ain't pay for shit on this side of town."

"I know this yo car bitch," I started counting to myself. I don't think she knew who she was dealing with. She swung the bat and busts my head light. "Robert I know you in there! Bring yo scared ass out!" and like on cue he come jogging out the house with his basketball shorts on, a white wife beater and his phomeposits. He bypassed me and went straight to Erica. There were so many people out there watching that the cars could barely pass by. Any other time the police wanted to drive back and forth up and down the street but at that moment none was in sight.

"Young, what the fuck is you doin young?" he asked.

"I called yo phone and you ain't answerin. What's up wit that?" her voice was annoying me.

"So what! You comin round here causin a scene and showin your ass tarin up people shit."

"Yeah and both ya'll weak asses gonna pay for my shit too!" I shouted. He snatched the bat from her and that was my chance to tax that ass. I ran up on her ready to pounce on her ass like a lion does its prey; but was pushed back by Rob.

"Rob move out my way for I beat yo ass too." She stood behind him scared for her life. She barked like a big dog but wasn't nothing but a lil ankle bitter.

"Yesi chill," Robert said so calm. His calmness was pissing me off in itself.

"What the fuck you mean chill? She bout to get this ass whoppin that's been waitin for her for awhile now."

"You not bout to fight her Yasmine damn," he had so much base in his voice.

"What the hell is goin on?" I heard Lisa say. I quickly looked back at her and seen that she was standing with Terrance. I raised my eyebrow at her then turned to look back at the two things of wasted space that stood before me.

"Jalissa come get yo friend and take her in the house." Robert said.

"I'm not goin nowhere, now move out my got damn way so I can whoop yo lil girlfriend ass."

"Go and tell her why she ain't bout to lay a finger on me Black," Erica said. Robert didn't say anything; he just looked around at the enormous crowd that formed. "Let her know that she ain't yo only babymama,"

"Umm," someone close in the crowd said.

"Yup, that's right; I'm pregnant. And we fucked in yo house on yo couch that's how I know where the fuck you stay."

"Daaaaaam!" someone else in the crowd yelled. My whole little world felt like it was crumbling down on me. I slapped Robert then reached around him punched Erica in the face and the back of her head when she tried to turn around. Robert quickly pulled me away from her. I wasn't going to beat her bad, just a little bit. Her stomach wouldn't have felt a thing.

"What you doin?" Robert asked furious. "She just told you she was pregnant!"

"The bitch face ain't pregnant." I screamed at him. I hated to be around Robert, he disgusted me. I drew my fist back and connected it to his jaw. "I hope you got bail money bitch cause you gonna have that baby in jail for fuckin up my got damn car!" I yelled as I heard the police sirens coming down the street. Robert tried to touch me and from that point on, everything just went black.

I felt so bad for Yesi, but I wanted to hit her with an *'I told you so,'* cause no one ever wants to listen to Joi. All those years he was cheating on her and the result was the young girl had gotten pregnant.

"Yesi, just come in the house and calm down." Lisa told her.

"How the fuck am I suppose to calm down? This red bitch fucked my car up." She began to breath heavy. "I swear I'm gonna kill yo fuckin cousin Lisa. Almost ten years, ten fuckin years and this shit that weak ass nigga wanna pull." And that was only half of the charades that went on. I was on my way to pick up Camille from my mom house when I got a call from Malikaa telling me to meet her at Yasmin's house and that it was an emergency. I rushed down Suitland Parkway and around the corner to Southern Avenue. I couldn't even make it to the front of her apartment building, so I parked three buildings down from hers. When I made it through the crowd of people my jaw dropped. Every window on Yasmine's car was broken out, even her headlights. It was a circus that I was ashamed to have been affiliated with. So many obscenities thrown left and right, everything was just so ghetto, hood and trashy; the whole situation. It took over an hour to get her to a point where she could be left alone. I left before everyone else, I had to go get my daughter and I hated being around South East after dark. I saw a familiar truck three cars before mine. I didn't want to seem nosy so I slowed down my pace, walking by the car slowly and glanced in it. I knew I knew that car. I walked up to the driver side window and tapped on it. Terrance looked at me then rolled his window down.

"Aye wassup Joi," he said with a lil smirk on his face.

"Hey Tee. What you doin out here?" I questioned curiously.

"Waitin on yo girl to finish handlin ya'll friend so we could go out to eat."

"Hmm," was all I got out. Last I knew they weren't talking anymore, not even on speaking terms; and now they going out on dates. "Ya'll still together, holdin strong I see,"

"Oh nah, we not together; just bout to go out, eat, and talk about the plans for Brandon."

"Oh wow what happened?" I was trying to pry my way into their business.

"She ain't tell you?"

"Nu uh, we don't talk like that anymore,"

"Just some mutual agreement; wasn't meant for us." I nodded my head.

"So her son is ya'll son," he nodded his head as well. "Now that I know I do see the resemblance. He's a handsome little boy." I truthfully told him.

"Thanks, well here come Lisa."

"That's my que. I'd see you around." I said then walked off towards my car. My phone rang in one of those generic ringtones that comes with the phone. I looked at it in my hand. It was Jamaal. I smiled; I'd call him back when I was settled in my car. I was in an unfamiliar neighborhood and wanted to have my full concentration on my surroundings. I plugged my phone into my car charger and dialed Jamaal's number back once I got comfortable in the car, ignition running and warming up.

"Hello?" He answered. My phone automatically connected to my car speakers when I entered the car.

"Hey baby, you called?" I loved talking to him. He listened, he gave his opinion and he had intelligent conversation. We were in this relationship without being in a relationship. He was my man and I was his woman, we just didn't make it to the sexual intimacy yet.

"Yeah, I ain't heard from you all day; I wanted to make sure you were okay." I smiled.

"Yes, I'm fine. I got a call from Malikaa telling me to come to the girl Yasmine house that I was telling you about. She said it was an emergency. I get over there and Yasmine and some young girl was fighting over Yasmine's boyfriend." I told him.

"Yasmine is the one with the boyfriend that was hitting on her," I knew all about Terrance and his hand problem. I was the one Lisa cried to when it first started, and I told her to leave him alone but her response was, *'I love him and he loves me. I just gotta figure out what I'm doin to make him so mad.'*

"No, that's Jalissa. Yasmine is the one who has the two kids and her baby daddy cheatin on her." I reminded him.

"Oh okay, so why was they fighting?"

"The mistress tore Yasmine's car up! And, and she's pregnant! The mistress."

"Damn,"

"Yeah, damn is right. They looked like a bunch of monkey's out there. It was so many people out to watch the show." I shook my head. "Anyway,"

"Yeah, so what you doin tonight?" he asked.

"I don't know, why?"

"I want to see you. Hold you. Kiss you." My love box began to tingle.

"Let me see if I can leave Camille with Darrell and I'll try to sneak out."

"Nah boo, spend some time with her. I'm gonna see you this weekend when we go out to Williamsburg." He planned for us to stay out in a hotel for the weekend. He said that I needed to relax and that he was going to take care of me like a man is suppose to.

"Okay," I pouted. I wasn't far from my mom's house, just around the corner. "Baby, I'm going to text you okay because I'm at my mom house and I'm going in to get Camille."

"Okay babe. Talk to you later,"

*

I kicked the door closed with my feet seeing that I had McDonald bags and cups in my hand. I really wanted Burger King but there was something about that golden arch that all kids love so much. Camille went running for the living room.

"Uh Camille get your butt back in here and take off those shoes." I told her. She traced her steps and came back and took off of her brown cowboy boots. She ran back into the living room then ran after me into the kitchen.

"Where daddy?" she asked. I shrugged my shoulders.

"I donno mama, I got here the same time as you." I told her. I tore the side of the McDonalds bag and started making her spread at her Tinker Bell table. "Come eat before your food get cold."

"But I want daddy eat wif me," she whined.

"What did I say?" she pouted and dragged her feet over to her little table. Her Tinker Bell table was the table that she eats at when I want to leave in and out of the kitchen and didn't have to worry about her touch or breaking anything on the dining room table and she'd be able to watch TV while she ate. I was ready to get out of my work clothes and relax myself. I started unbuttoning my shirt before I hit the steps. I stopped midway up the stairs just listening. I heard something tapping the wall. Faint grunting sounds coming from up there. My heart was pounding fast. I started my walk up the stairs again and the closer I got to my bedroom door the louder those grunting sounds were. The louder that tapping sound was. I was praying for his sake and my sanity that he was busting a nut to a porno.

My door wasn't a silent one when it was opened, so my presence was known when I opened the door. Darrell stopped mid stroke. Stephanie bent over at the receiving end of his back shots. And when I say back shots, I ment them. There were two sets of balls in that room, and two dicks harder than the concrete outside that house. I couldn't say anything. I was so disgusted. Darrell pulled out and hurriedly put his boxers on. Stephanie, or was its real name Stephen? Whatever it was slowly took its time dressing, starring at me making sure I wasn't going to hurdle over Darrell and knock the head off its shoulders.

"Joi, baby let me explain." He took a step towards me I took one back. I put my hand up signaling for him to shut up.

"You brought this, this," I was at lost for words, "this thing into our house. Made me cook and have dinner with it. Then," I had to stop myself because tears were threatening to pour out of my eyes any minute.

"Joi I'm so sorry," I gave a sarcastic laugh as tears glossed my eyes.

"You're fuckin a man Darrell! How the fuck can I compete with that?" I shouted at him. "I can't accept your apology, take you back and learn new fuckin tricks to try and keep you interested. You weren't interested in the first fuckin place."I held my thumb and pointer finger between my eyes. "I'm so fuckin stupid," I said more to myself.

"Mommy, I don't want no more." I looked up and seen Camille on the last step coming towards us.

"Go back down stairs baby, I'm coming." I told her. I guess she seen Darrell body in the door way so she began to run to us. "Camille, I said go back down stairs." I said stopping her in mid stride. She pouted.

"But I want my daddy,"

"What did I just tell yo ass?" I shouted. "Take yo hard headed butt back downstairs." She jumped and turned on her heels. I started to follow her when he, Darrell grabbed my arm. I turned around and swung on him. I continued to swing on him until I finally hit him one good time in the face.

"I hate yo ass Darrell. You have nothin to say to me and it's nothin you could do to fix this!" he looked at me so pitiful. "Jamaal was tryin to tell me, he really was. And I *knew* you were fuckin around, I just wanted evidence and this was just a slap in the face."I seen as he kept mumbling Jamaal trying to figure out who that was.

"Yes Jamaal, your partner at the firm. We have been dating for a few months now. Unlike you, I took my marriage a little more serious than you. We didn't fuck. Although I shoulda told you that we did so I could see a little more hurt and pain in yo eyes, just like what I'm feelin."

"Joi—" I didn't want to hear anything and I mean *anything* he had to say out of his mouth. I turned on my heels and left. I went downstairs grabbed a crying Camille off of the last step go our coats and purse put both of our shoes on and stormed out the door making sure to slam it behind me.

Jalissa

I sat stood next to Terrance as we waited in the ridiculously long line to get into Chuck E' Cheese. As old as I was I always was excited to spend a few hours in the place where an adult can be a kid. I stuffed my hands in my pockets as Brandon stood in front of me leaning on my legs. He had a tendency to do that when we were waiting in line. I felt Terrance nudge me on the side. I looked at him.

"What's wrong with you?" I shook my head. "This not about last night is it?" I shook my head. "Lisa?"

"I don't wanna talk about it right now Tee." I told him. He looked at me but didn't press the issue. The night when we went out ended in one big mistake. Corey and I weren't officially back together but we were working on something's. Terrance took me out to Olive Garden. He knew pasta was my favorite. We had a great time talking over dinner. We got caught up on what was going on in each other's lives. Not once did we bring up or dwell on our past. He reminded me why I had fallen in love with him the first time around. After we left Olive

Garden we went to a bar around the corner from the restaurant. I started off with a tequila sunrise and after that the drinks just kept coming and coming. We laughed, joked around and drank. I woke up in his bed under his arm. I could smack myself for waking up in his bed.

"What the hell?" I said as I sat up in his bed. I grabbed my head from the headache that I was brewing. He stairred in his sleep. "I'm so fuckin stupid." I moved his arm away from me and got out of bed in search of my clothes.

"What you doin?" he asked peeking at me with one eye open. I pulled my phone out of my coat pocket. It was a quarter to eleven. I had a missed call and text from Corey.

"Umm, I need to get home to Brandon." I said as I wiggled my way into my jeans. He lift up, propping himself up on his pillows. He rubbed his hands over his tired face.

"Aight," he didn't question me, he just got up and began to get ready. So I stood in line uncomfortable as ever and ready to get the day over with.

Brandon eyes lit up once he seen all the games, and lights. He tried to pull me to where all the games were.

"Hold on baby, let mommy get you some tokens."I told him. I pulled him in the direction of the token machine. Terrance was already there filling a cup up with tokens.

"Go head and find us a table. I'll take him out to the games." He told me. I nodded my head and bent down to Brandon's level. I started taking off his coat and hat.

"Be good for daddy okay?" he just looked at me with a blank stare. "You hear me?" he nodded his head. I stood up and left the two to go and spend some father and son time. It took me fifteen minutes to actually get a table. People acted like they wanted to stay in there all day not wanting to leave. I hawked a table until the people got up. I never did call or text Corey after seeing that he tried to get in touch with me. I pulled my phone out and texted him.

To: Baby
Sent: Wednesday, October 23, 2012
1:50pm
Hey baby, wat u doin

To: Lisa
Sent: Wednesday, October 23, 2012
1:55pm
Sittin @ my cuz house bored as duck.

Fuck damn auto correct*

When yall comin home?

To: Baby
Sent: Wednesday, October 23, 2012
1:56pm
Lol. We leavin in the mornin

To: Lisa
Sent: Wednesday, October 23, 2012
1:59pm
ok.

What's the deal when u get home

To: Baby
Sent: Wednesday, October 23, 2012

2:10pm

we startin from scratch right? So that's what we doin, u not comin back til we get back to that point in the relationship.

To: Lisa

Sent: Wednesday, October 23, 2012

2:15pm

ight lisa.

*

An hour later and a bucket filled with tickets later Brandon and Terrance came back to the table smiling. I smiled back at them. I never realized how much they looked alike until they were in my face side by side.

"Ya'll have fun?" I asked. I went and played a few games but I really wasn't into it for some reason. I was just tired and ready to go home and have a good sleep in my own bed.

"Mommy look what all tickets Tawence got me." I smiled.

"I see!" I said in his same exciting tone. "What you gonna get with all those tickets?"

"Candy," I chuckled. I looked up over at Terrance as

he sat down. He looked worn out.

"Bran come sit and eat some pizza before you go back out there." I told him I had ordered pizza about twenty minutes before they came over. I sat him inside of the booth and cut him up a slice of pizza.

"So, ya'll leave tomorrow," He stated rather than asked.

"Yeah, I can't wait to go home and get in my own bed." I told him. I rubbed my hands on my thighs.

"What we gonna do about B once ya'll leave?"

"I thought we discussed that last night,"

"We did, but something else happened and I forgot what it was we were talking about." I turned a light shade of red. "so about last night,"

"It shouldn't of happened. That's a road I am not goin back down with you Terrance." I told him. He said nothing more of it. "I'll bring Brandon back down for all the major Holidays. And we can talk about you keepin him for the summer." I told him.

"You never told me when his birthday,"

"May fifteenth."

*

"We'll be back down for Thanksgiving. If we don't make it down for that we'll defiantly be down for Christmas." I told Terrance as he stood outside my car. It was six o'clock in the morning and I was preparing to get back on the road to head back up to Chicago. Terrance insisted that he seen us off. He pulled me into a hug; I didn't let the hug last more than ten seconds.

"Aight," he said. "You gonna give me some contact info so I could stay in touch with my son?"

"I thought I gave it to you," I knew I didn't. I reached in my car and ripped a piece of paper off of a sheet of paper that I didn't need and wrote my number on it.

"Address?" he said.

"Uh no, just the number for now." I told him.

"Aight," he looked in the back seat at a sleeping Brandon. "Have my lil man call me when he get up."

"Okay,"

"And I'm serious Jalissa, don't have my son callin that nigga of yours daddy," I sucked my teeth.

"Aight Terrance. And I'll have Brandon call you when he wakes up," I told him. He stepped back away from the car so that I could get in.

"Aight man, ya'll be safe on the road. And at least

text me when you get back to Chicago." I arched my eyebrow at how he knew where I was staying. "I know the area code." I rolled my eyes at him.

"Bye Terrance." I shut the door and he watched me until I pulled off.

Yasmine

My heart was broken in a million and one pieces. It's like, I knew he was messing with that girl and I could deal with that. But he went and got her pregnant; that was something I couldn't deal with. That mean I would have to interact with her, and even if he told me for the guzillionth time that he wasn't fucking her I knew he'd be lying. Because everyone knows that at least for the first year of that baby life they were going to be dipping and dabbing. Most have done it. That baby wasn't here yet and I already knew that I would have some resentment against him; or her. That child and its mother was the cause of my failed relationship. I was thankful for insurance because within a week I had a new car while the shop repaired my old one. Everyone thought that break up with Robert was temporary, some thought he was gonna break me; but not once did I cry in his presence. I may have let the water works began once I closed that door but he was not going to ever see me shed a tear over him again. My phone blew up with calls from him, and then he tried to call me from unknown numbers. I knew it was him because everyone that calls my number is saved in my phone. Him and that girl was made for each other. Both young minded, no job, and dumb as fuck. Sit around and smoke blunts all day, if that's what they wanted to do then yeah, she could have him.

I pulled up inside of Burger Kings parking lot hungry as hell. I was on my way to go and pick up Isaac and Xavier from school, but wanted to stop and get me something to eat before getting them. I could have waited until he I picked them up, but I didn't have the money to get all of us something from there and plus I planned on cooking dinner. Not paying attention when I got out the car I bumped into someone. I looked up to say I'm sorry and fell deep inside these hypnotizing hazel orbs. I smiled up at him.

"My bad," I said.

"You aight," he told me. "What's yo name?"

"Yesi," I smiled. He did the same, his teeth so perfect and white. His complexion so chocolate, perfect toned body.

"Ezekiel," he extended his hand. I shook it.

"Nice to meet you; uh, I'm sorry I can't sit and

chat but I'm runnin late getting my kids from school." I told him.

"No problem. I guess if I see you again I'd be able to get your number," he smirked. I did the same and agreed with him.

I got to the boys school and rushed inside. I wasn't late picking them up. I just wanted to beat the traffic getting out of the school parking lot. The school was a one way in and one way out. Why did they do it that way, hell if I knew.

"You must be stalkin me," I heard newly familiar voice say behind me. I turned around and laughed. Must be faith telling me to move my ass on.

"Nah, you stalkin me." I told him. "What you followed me?"

"Nah, nah, I'm coming to get my son as a matter of fact," he said.

"Umm, okay."

"And to get your number so I can take you out to dinner." He added. I blushed.

"Hmm, well let start off with you giving me your number and I'll call you and let you know if I'm interested in going to dinner with you." I told him.

"I guess that'll work," he said. I pulled out my phone so I could store his number in my phone. We sat and got a little information out of each other while we waited for the kids to come out. Single dad to a seven year old; worked at a barber shop off Southern Avenue, own car, apartment. That's what I needed. A man, a real man to step to the plate. Maybe Ezekiel was that dark and handsome guy to swoop me off my feet. Only time could tell.

Malikaa

Rashaad practically lived at my house he had clothes there and I even gave him a spare key. I was trying to ease my way away from Darious, but he still called me every day, texted me every ten minutes. Don't get me wrong, I still had those deep, *deep* feelings for him but I was in love with Rashaad. I wanted things to work out with us. I still dipped back in the Darious jar from time to time; and every time I went back he asked,

"Where you been?"

"I'm trying to get things together in my life. You know I haven't talked to Joi in a month? I went to her house and Darrell sayin that he ain't talk to her nor has she been home."

"Damn, she ain't do a M.I.A. on us like Jalissa, did she?" he asked.

"Lawd I hope not." That was the last conversation we had before clawing each other's clothes off.

I really hope she didn't. I couldn't take another few months of worrying if she was dead or alive. What I didn't get was the fact that Darrell acted like he didn't care. Not a sad or worried bone in his body. I was so relieved when she called me, asking me to meet her at the Ihop in New Carrolton. I couldn't get their fast enough. She sounded so down, not the Joi I was use to. I walked into the restaurant and looked around for her. I didn't see her so I called.

"Where you at?" I asked.

"I'm in the back by where the bathrooms are."

"Okay," I ended our call and walked in the direction of where she told me. I spotted her and Camille sitting in a booth. Camille was sipping out of her pink sippy cup. I eased my way into the booth with them.

"Hey honey," I said to Joi.

"Hi Aunt Meme!" Camille said excitedly.

"Hey Camy baby! What you been up to?" she shrugged.

"Me and mommy been on a vacation in a hotel with a pool." She loved to swim.

"You had fun?"

"Uh huh, I swim all night." I smiled her then focused my attention on Joi. Her sigh was so heavy and deep. She pulled out her phone and some headphones.

"Camille, watch Tinker Bell movie while I talked to Meme." She said as she put the headphones in her ears. She threw her head in her hands.

"What's wrong?" I asked her.

"My whole world is falling apart. I was supposed to be the one in this perfect relationship, wonderful life." She looked at me with tears streaming down her face.

"What happened? Why you crying?" I reached over and rubbed her arms trying to calm her down.

"I told you that bastard was cheatin on me; with that damn Stephanie character," My mouth dropped. I couldn't believe what I was hearing. "That's not the worst part Malikaa,"

"Oh my God, I'm scared to hear,"

"That Stephanie bitch is a fuckin man," my jaw dropped. "I caught them in the the middle of fuckin, dick and balls everywhere." It was not a time to laugh but that statement was funny.

"You gotta go get tested Joi," she shook her head no. "What you mean no?"

"I can't I don't want to know if it's something bad." She told me.

"You need to know so you can get treated if something does pop up." I told her. "I'll go with you. Hell, I'll get test with you."

"Malikaa, what if he gave me something?" she sounded so scared.

"I'll help you kill him," I tried to throw a joke in there. She was not having it. "I'm just playing. We'll get through it." I told her. She just nodded her head and looked over at Camille. She was scared.

*

I held my results in my hand my leg shook in anger tears streamed down my face. Why the hell did I volunteer to get the damn AIDs test with her? While she walked around with a test that gave her great life I tried to figure out when my life took a turn for the worst. I was going to literally kill Rashaad when I got back home. He went and stuck his dick in some AIDs infested man in jail and brought that shit home to me. I was so pissed that I couldn't cry. I walked in my house and slammed the door. Rashaad jumped up from lying on the couch. I stormed over to him and threw my results at him.

"Get yo shit and get the hell out my house." I yelled at him. He read over the paper and his face flashed red. Anger covered his face.

"Positive Malikaa?" he said, voice filled with rage.

"That's what the fuck it says Rashaad. I can't fuckin believe you! I can't believe I trusted you that much!"

"I didn't give you that shit, I make sure strap up. You better check that nigga you been fuckin," he yelled. He was moving around the house gathering his stuff. He went over and got a trash bag out of the cabinet. He was throwing everything he owned in there.

"I am, you got a lot of explain to do."

"Nah, I ain't talkin bout me. I'm talkin bout that nigga you been leavin for the weekend with. The one you was fuckin while I was locked up."

"I ain't fuckin no body but you,"

"Yeah, okay Malikaa. If you were waitin for me for that year your shit shoulda been tight. Yo pussy was just too loose for you to have been faithful." Once he was done he threw my key on the table and left. Not a bye, fuck you; nothing. I picked up my phone and called Darious. I tried to sound as calm as possible. As soon as he said 'hello,' I asked him to come over. Within thirty minutes Darious was at my house and sitting on my couch. I handed him my results letter.

"Why Darious?" He just continued to look at the letter. "I trusted you,"

"Damn," he rubbed his head over his faced. He looked at me with sincere eyes. "I'm sorry Malikaa,"

"There's no amount of sorry's that can fix this! I have to live with this shit for the rest of my life!" I was so pissed off. More at myself than anything.

"We can get through it. There's medicine you can take,"

"Darious, you make it seem like you planned this shit. You don't just go around fuckin people passing that shit around like it's a cup of water. This is something you should have told me before we got to the point of having sex. It's my decision if I wanted to go on and risk my health."

"And I know that Malikaa, but it is what it is now. Like I said the only thing we can do is work things out. I'll let you know of the places to go and help you out." I was in so much rage. I didn't want him to leave this house without some type of wundes on him. I wanted to take my sharpest knife and pierce his hart. I jumped on him and continuously hit him in his face, in his chest, tears falling freely from my eyes. I tried to wrap my hands his thick ass neck but he held me at my wrist.

"Malikaa, calm down," he had the audacity to tell me.

"Get out my house, I don't wanna talk to you, I don't wanna see your face. If you contact me I will go to the police." I told him. He tried so hard to protest but I couldn't sit and listen to anything he had to say. I always said, you reap what you sow; and I was reaping this big ass seed.

To be continued…

16241060R00090

Made in the USA
Charleston, SC
11 December 2012